Affect, Consciousness and Self

This book argues that mental life is organized by and around affect. It proposes a clinical model for understanding how affect influences states of consciousness and self. It illustrates how, from moment to moment, affect determines the world we know, how we are disposed to being in it, and our capacity to function in it.

After introducing consciousness and self as features of the mind that have posed daunting problems for philosophy, neurology, and psychoanalysis, subsequent chapters propose a model for understanding them at the clinical level. The initial chapters are devoted to the influence of affect on the structure and dynamics of normal waking consciousness and on the self's capacity to act agentically, to relate intersubjectively, and to develop itself. The final chapters discuss disordered states of consciousness and impeded self-functioning due to affect dysregulation, and what all this looks like in patients with preoccupied and avoidant attachment patterns.

Drawing on psychoanalysis, attachment theory, interpersonal and affective neurobiology, and traumatology, this book offers a fresh perspective on the importance of affect for psychoanalysts and psychodynamic psychotherapists.

Daniel Hill is a psychoanalyst and educator. He is the author of *Affect Regulation Theory: A Clinical Model* and is on the faculties of the National Institute of the Psychotherapies and the New York University Postdoctoral Program in Psychoanalysis and Psychotherapy.

Relational Perspectives Book Series

RBP

The Relational Perspectives Book Series (RPBS) publishes books that grow out of or contribute to the relational tradition in contemporary psychoanalysis. The term *relational psychoanalysis* was first used by Greenberg and Mitchell[1] to bridge the traditions of interpersonal relations, as developed within interpersonal psychoanalysis and object relations, as developed within contemporary British theory. But, under the seminal work of the late Stephen A. Mitchell, the term *relational psychoanalysis* grew and began to accrue to itself many other influences and developments. Various tributaries—interpersonal psychoanalysis, object relations theory, self psychology, empirical infancy research, feminism, queer theory, sociocultural studies and elements of contemporary Freudian and Kleinian thought—flow into this tradition, which understands relational configurations between self and others, both real and fantasied, as the primary subject of psychoanalytic investigation.

We refer to the relational tradition, rather than to a relational school, to highlight that we are identifying a trend, a tendency within contemporary psychoanalysis, not a more formally organized or coherent school or system of beliefs. Our use of the term *relational* signifies a dimension of theory and practice that has become salient across the wide spectrum of contemporary psychoanalysis. Now under the editorial supervision of Adrienne Harris and Eyal Rozmarin, the Relational Perspectives Book Series originated in 1990 under the editorial eye of the late Stephen A. Mitchell. Mitchell was the most prolific and influential of the originators of the relational tradition. Committed to dialogue among psychoanalysts, he abhorred the authoritarianism that dictated adherence to a rigid set of beliefs or technical restrictions. He championed open discussion, comparative and integrative approaches, and promoted new voices across the generations. Mitchell was later joined by the late Lewis Aron, also a visionary and influential writer, teacher, and leading thinker in relational psychoanalysis.

Included in the Relational Perspectives Book Series are authors and works that come from within the relational tradition, those that extend and develop that tradition, and works that critique relational approaches or compare and contrast them with alternative points of view. The series includes our most distinguished senior psychoanalysts, along with younger contributors who bring fresh vision. Our aim is to enable a deepening of relational thinking while reaching across disciplinary and social boundaries in order to foster an inclusive and international literature.

A full list of titles in this series is available at https://www.routledge.com/Relational-Perspectives-Book-Series/book-series/LEARPBS.

Note

1 Greenberg, J., & Mitchell, S. (1983). *Object relations in psychoanalytic theory.* Cambridge, MA: Harvard University Press.

Affect, Consciousness and Self

The View from the Bottom of the Mind

Daniel Hill

Routledge
Taylor & Francis Group

LONDON AND NEW YORK

Designed cover image: Ezra Bassin-Hill (2024)

First published 2025
by Routledge
4 Park Square, Milton Park, Abingdon, Oxon OX14 4RN

and by Routledge
605 Third Avenue, New York, NY 10158

Routledge is an imprint of the Taylor & Francis Group, an informa business

© 2026 Daniel Hill

British Library Cataloguing-in-Publication Data
A catalogue record for this book is available from the British Library

Library of Congress Cataloging-in-Publication Data
Names: Hill, Daniel (Psychologist), author.
Title: Affect, consciousness and self: a view from the bottom
of the mind / Daniel Hill.
Description: Abingdon, Oxon; New York, NY: Routledge, 2025. |
Series: Relational perspectives |
Includes bibliographical references and index. |
Identifiers: LCCN 2024060992 (print) | LCCN 2024060993 (ebook) |
ISBN 9781032210735 (pbk) | ISBN 9781032210728 (hbk) |
ISBN 9781003266617 (ebk)
Subjects: LCSH: Affect (Psychology) | Consciousness. |
Affective neuroscience.
Classification: LCC BF175.5.A35 H54 2025 (print) |
LCC BF175.5.A35 (ebook) | DDC 152.4—dc23/eng/20250321
LC record available at https://lccn.loc.gov/2024060992
LC ebook record available at https://lccn.loc.gov/2024060993

ISBN: 978-1-032-21072-8 (hbk)
ISBN: 978-1-032-21073-5 (pbk)
ISBN: 978-1-003-26661-7 (ebk)

DOI: 10.4324/9781003266617

Typeset in Times New Roman
by codeMantra

To my teachers and students
and
To My Nina

Contents

Preface and Acknowledgments

My first in-depth encounter with a psychological theory was with Piaget's theory of cognitive development. He argued that the cognitive operations of the mind emerged from the actions of the body. They developed from sensorimotor, to preoperational, to concrete operations, to formal operations—increasingly adaptive schemas for understanding space, time, and causality. I next encountered Freud and ego psychology. In this case, the mind was understood to emerge out of the need to regulate the drives (the body) and again the concern was adaptation, this time to internal and external environments. The problem with ego psychology was its theory psychosexual development and pathogenesis did not hold up to the criticisms they were up against. I next learned object relations theory and self psychology, and, because I was trained at the New York University Postdoctoral Program in Psychoanalysis and Psychotherapy, the relational school of psychoanalysis was exploding all around me. Each school of thought was filled with clinical acumen and illuminated crucial aspects of mental life. The problem for me was their neglect of the primacy of the body. In the early 2000's, I encountered Schore's affect regulation theory which sees the mind as emerging from the body's need to survive by adapting to its internal and external environments. Most of our trainings did not include attachment theory, traumatology, or neurobiology all of which were necessary to understand affect regulation theory. My previous book is meant to serve as a textbook for those wishing to learn it.

My aim in writing this book is to expand regulation theory to include an understanding of how consciousness and the self are organized by affect. The project emerged as I was coming to appreciate that thinking about the mind in terms of implicit and explicit processes provides a more differentiated and comprehensive understanding of mental life than understanding the mind as divided simply into unconscious and conscious processes. I came to see how implicit and explicit processes assemble qualitatively different states of consciousness that present us with different worlds and dispose us to different ways of being in them. I also came to see that these processes enable the self to perform very different kinds of functions. I had learned from regulation theory that our affect state determines the extent to which implicit and explicit processes are available to us. I saw that, ultimately, affect determines the world we're in what we're capable of doing while in it.

My interest in theory and especially in clinical models originates with my teachers and mentors: John Sullivan, Elazar Pedhazur, Bernie Kalinkowitz, Fred Pine, Norbert Freedman, and Manny Ghent. As with my previous book, my indebtedness to Allan Schore is profound. His theory of affect regulation reorientated my thinking completely and conversations with him have been invaluable. The ideas for the model presented here were forged in conversations with members of my study groups and courses I've taught. I also shared early drafts of these chapters with them, and their reactions have been invaluable and led to many changes. They are Beverly Brisk, Amy Gladstone, Beth Sandweiss, Claire Ciliotta, Debby Russ, Janice Rosenman, Susan Markowitz, and Susan Parente; Clair Goldberg, Deborah Kaplan, Karen Greenberg, Margot Schwartz, Naomi Fox, Rosemarie Ciccarello, Sarah Karl, and Susan Levine; Carol Antler, Kenneth Greenwald, and Satya Lauren; Ashley Leeds, Maria Rappaport, Nina Sander, and Vincent Handon. Friends and colleagues Peter Deri, Robert Karen, and Peter Kaufmann offered invaluable help. I am also appreciative of the editorial staff at Routledge, Deepika Batra and Kate Hawes, who were patient and helpful throughout the process. And I am endlessly grateful to my partner, Nina Cohen, without whom this book would not be what it is.

Introduction: Affect, Consciousness, and Self

A Clinical Model

Introduction

Over the past 30 years, fundamental changes have occurred in psychoanalysis. There has been increasing agreement that affect is primary and that the mind is organized by it, there has been growing appreciation of the clinical importance of consciousness, and there has been a refinement in our understanding of the mind. The simple distinction between conscious and unconscious processes is being replaced with more differentiated distinctions between implicit and explicit processes. They are different kinds of processes that serve different functions. This book proposes a clinically oriented model of mind reflecting these changes.

My previous book (Hill, 2015) was meant to serve as a primer for Allan Schore's theories of affect regulation and interpersonal neurobiology. It focused on the unconscious processes that regulate affect and on the foundational role of affect in psychological development, pathogenesis, and therapeutic action. In this book, I apply these ideas to illustrate the role of affect in organizing consciousness and the self. The model I will propose depicts a mind comprised of implicit and explicit processes. They construct consciousness, the world we know, and they determine what the self experiences, what it can do, and what it is disposed to do. These processes are organized by affect. The model is an integration of the work of Antonio Damasio (1994, 1999, 2010), Gerald Edelman[1] (1989, 2004), Peter Fonagy[2] (2002, 2016), Russell Meares[3] (2005, 2012a, 2012b, 2016), Ian McGilchrist[4] (2009), and Allan Schore[5] (1994, 2003a, 2003b, 2012, 2019a, 2019b).

In Chapter 1, I provide a review of affect regulation theory and discuss the primacy of affect. In Chapter 2, I provide a clinically oriented model of consciousness in which shifts of affect states generate shifts in states of

DOI: 10.4324/9781003266617-1

consciousness. In Chapter 3, I provide a model of a core self that serves as the locus and shaper of experience and as the performer of functions. In Chapter 4, I provide a model of how dysregulated affect induces disorders of consciousness and impedes the functioning of the self. In Chapter 5, I apply the model to the clinical understanding of insecurely attached patients. Some readers may prefer to read this chapter first.

Consciousness and Self: Daunting Problems

Consciousness: Let me begin with just how far we are from understanding fundamental aspects of consciousness. It's famous for being the last great mystery and for being a topic one dares not pursue until after one has tenure. McGilchrist (2009) notes that part of the difficulty is that there is nothing analogous to consciousness, nothing with its sense of innerness. Traditionally, the study of consciousness fell to philosophy. After generations of frustration, philosophers turned to neuroscience for help, but it too has come up against daunting obstacles. Take, for example, the so-called "hard problem." How does the brain produce consciousness and, most fundamentally, how does the matter of the brain produce something that seems to be nonmatter?

Edelman (1989) argues that consciousness is an emergent phenomenon that arises out of the increasing complexity of neural processes spread throughout the brain. There is widespread agreement that no one neural structure produces consciousness and that it originates subcortically at the level of the brain stem. Most importantly for what follows, there is agreement that the consciousness we come into the world with is constructed by the right brain, and the complexity of consciousness develops along with the increasing complexity of the brain. Each step along the way toward maximum complexity improves the capacity of the organism to survive (Damasio, 1999; Panksepp, 2004, 2012; Solms, 2021).

The idea that consciousness is linked to the complexity of the brain has led some to posit that computers will be capable of consciousness once they gain sufficient complexity (see, e.g., Dennett, 1991). However, most agree with Edelman (1989), Damasio (1999, 2010), and Solms (2021) that consciousness requires a body; that affective experience, the felt sense of the body changing, was the spark that turned on the lights[6]; and that consciousness originates in affect.[7]

If these ideas about the production of consciousness prove correct, that consciousness is an emergent phenomenon that originates in affect, we are still faced with the even more daunting, second part of the problem. How does brain matter produce the seeming immateriality of consciousness? We have no idea. We're left with this. If consciousness is not matter, science can have nothing to say about it. If consciousness is some form of matter, science remains at a loss to know what that matter is.

Another formidable, more clinically relevant problem is that consciousness is a private affair experienced by and known only to its owner. What is it like for you when you see blue? The same experience as when I see blue? This is known as the "qualia problem" and is at the heart of understanding consciousness as "...a mind endowed with subjectivity" (Damasio, 2010, p. 4). Those attempting to solve the qualia problem are up against the position of the philosopher Thomas Nagel (1974) who, in a paper entitled "What Is It Like to Be a Bat?" argued that knowing another's consciousness is impossible, empirically, or otherwise. While there are objective signs of whether consciousness is off or on (It's an "off-on" phenomenon.), no way has been found to measure the subjective experience of it. William James (2001) argued that introspection is the only way to study it. Like the problems of what consciousness is and how it's made, the qualia problem has been intractable.

Most who study consciousness agree that we're not the only species equipped with it. While it's generally thought that plants don't have it, and it's arguable whether insects, birds, and lizards do, most agree that mammals are likely to have the basic form of consciousness in which they are aware of their existence in the present. Edelman called it "primary consciousness." A later developing second level of consciousness called "reflective consciousness" is a mark of homosapien that allows them all manner of advantages including an awareness of the past and future. Only a few of the other later developing apes, such as chimpanzees and bonobos, are believed to have it, and it's clear that theirs is far less complex than ours.

Damasio (1999) outlines a fascinating series of evolutionary developments leading to the advent of organisms, and then organisms with a mind capable of representing objects but operating in the dark, and then with a mind equipped with primary consciousness, and then reflective consciousness.[8] With each step, we became better at assessing the adaptive value of objects and better at responding to them adaptively. This progression puts consciousness in its place—a very late add-on to the body and in its service.

Again, the first kind of consciousness to develop, phylogenetically and ontogenetically, is called primary consciousness. It is the simple awareness of our perceptions and of the existence of ourselves experiencing them—a simple phenomenological awareness of the present, no past or future. One is conscious of oneself in the present responding to objects. Without the capacity to reflect, we respond to objects automatically, simply stimulus-response, without agency. Eventually homeo sapiens developed a second level of consciousness allowing us to reflect on the primary level. It changed everything.

Reflective consciousness begins to develop during the second year of life. We develop the capacity to conjure an inner world where we can re-present things that we've perceived in the past and perform mental operations on those mental representations.[9] With this comes the capacity to direct our thoughts. We are no longer simply a stimulus-response machine trapped in the present. Equipped with a representational world, we can think about the past and future. We develop a temporal perspective. We can anticipate and plan. We can think about what we want to have happen and direct our actions toward that goal. Agency, acting intentionally, becomes possible. From a phylogenetic point of view, once reflective consciousness emerged, in the blink of an evolutionary eye, we went from an inconsequential, sophisticated ape, surviving by hunting and gathering in small groups, to Earth's dominant species. It was a cognitive revolution that led to complex social structures, science, morality,[10] culture, narrative, individual identities, and personal meaning (Damasio, 1999; Edelman, 2004).

Given its historical focus on the unconscious, it is perhaps not surprising that psychoanalysis has no theory of consciousness. Until recently, psychoanalysis accepted Freud's simple distinction between conscious and unconscious processes. There was little interest in the former except that consciousness was the way out of being governed by one's past. Janet, however, observed *levels* of consciousness. He understood them to be essential to understanding the conversion symptoms exhibited by his hysterical patients (Crapara & Ortu, 2019; Janet, 1901). He coined the term "*sub*conscious" (*sous conscieux*) to refer to the lower, "narrowed" state of consciousness to which his patients regressed when traumatic memories were activated[11] (Ellenberger, 1970). His understanding of such constricted states of consciousness were the first studies of disordered consciousness. They occurred when his patients were severely dysregulated due to the activation of traumatic memories. Since then, the psychoanalytic study of consciousness has made steady, albeit slow progress.

Rappaport (1951) became concerned with fluctuations in the quality of conscious thinking, especially with whether or not there was a reflective capacity. Broad advances began when Hartman (1958) extended psychoanalysis to include external adaptation and thereby established consciousness as an essential concern. Ego psychologists became interested in states of consciousness which they called "ego states." Winnicott's (1971) ideas about transitional states of consciousness became crucial to our understanding of development, play, and therapeutic action. Fonagy and his colleagues (2002, 2016) established mentalization theory and the importance of reflective consciousness for agency and for intersubjectivity. Finally, Tronick (1998, 2004) and Rosegrant (2005) have identified states of consciousness that are intrinsically growth promoting. The psychoanalytic concern with consciousness has advanced to the point where Fonagy asserts that "…seeing consciousness merely as a route to concerns outside awareness underestimates its role in the dynamics of mind and clinical psychoanalysis" (Crapparo & Mucci, 2017, p. XII).

Building on Janet's work, attention also turned to understanding disordered consciousness as a factor in psychopathology. Bromberg (1998, 2006) included dissociated states of consciousness in his understanding of enactment. Shane (2018) argued that levels of consciousness are "foundational for understanding the impact of trauma on brain development and function." Maroda (2020) urged that enactments would be better understood in terms of levels of consciousness rather than, simply, as unconscious versus conscious processes. Fonagy and Allison (2016) note that reflective consciousness is a "developmental achievement" and is "…vulnerable to experiences of neglect and maltreatment" (p. 5). Bach (1985) brought attention to the disordered states of consciousness due to a lack of balance between "subjective awareness" and "objective awareness" (aka subject consciousness and object consciousness). I have depicted different types of disordered consciousness that accompany different types of affect dysregulation and argued that we need a better understanding of disordered consciousness to appreciate our patients' subjective experience and for them to appreciate what happens to them when dysregulated (Hill, 2021).

The Self: And what of the self in my title? Before beginning with that discussion, we need first to come to grips with an important and disorienting idea. Consciousness and the self are two ways of looking at the same thing.

Ramachandran (2004) puts it that they are "two sides of the same coin." Perhaps their coincidence should be obvious. After all, consciousness requires a self who does the knowing and experiencing, and to exist the self must be conscious. The self disappears, for example, during dreamless sleep and under anesthesia. We also see the correspondence of consciousness and self in the fact that one is hard-pressed to distinguish between consciousness and subjective experience.

For our purposes, the best way to think about the coincidence of consciousness and self is that they are both features of the mind and that the mind is comprised of implicit and explicit processes. When those processes organize awareness, we call it "consciousness." When they perform adaptive functions and when they contribute to subjective experience, we think in terms of the self.[12] The point is that consciousness and self are comprised of the same stuff—implicit and explicit processes.

The conceptualization of the self has been elusive. Part of the problem is our insistence on reifying "it." The self is not a thing. It is systems of processes (Emde, 1983). There is no entity "in there" looking out from behind our eyes. The "homunculus" is an illusion. Searles (2008) notes that if there were a homunculus in there, it would also have to have a homunculus in there and so on ad infinitum. Let me add one more thought. This entity that we imagine in there is so filled with its own importance that it assumes that the body is there to house it; that the body is there for its benefit. It turns out that the opposite is the case. The self is a late forming addition to the mind which was a late forming addition to the body. It came packaged with consciousness. It evolved because, like consciousness, it improved the body's adaptive capacities, and thus, its chances of surviving and thriving.

That the self is an illusion shouldn't surprise us. There are no things in the mind. Nevertheless, accepting the idea that the self is a figment of our imagination has proven to be difficult. Add it to the heap of narcissistic insults delivered by Galileo that we're not at the center of the universe, by Darwin that we're not a thing apart from other creatures, and by Freud that we don't have free will. This, however, is the ultimate blow—we don't exist!

While the self is an illusion, it's a useful one. It helps us make sense of it all. It grounds us in our bodies and serves as a center for the knower, experiencer, and doer. It provides the sense of a concrete object to love and hate, and to be the star of the movie in our head that we call consciousness. And, of course, like many illusions, the homunculus is a comfort. Finally, regarding the usefulness of reification, "the" self is a handy way to refer to systems of implicit and explicit processes that assemble consciousness, generate subjective experience, and perform functions. So, for the sake of ease, I'll continue to refer to "*the* self."

Psychoanalysis is no exception when it comes to the elusiveness of a conceptualization of the self. Meares (2005) notes that Jung, Sullivan, and Kohut, major psychoanalytic theoreticians of the self, never defined it. We can add Winnicott, Mahler, Daniel Stern, and Fonagy to the group. Nevertheless, without defining it generally, theoreticians have described facets of the self that have become part and parcel of clinical practice: the true and false selves, the subjective self, the experiencing self, the observing self, the child self, the agentic self, the narrative self, the inner and outward self, self-states, etc.

Two theorists who did define the self are central to the model I'm proposing. Allan Schore conceptualizes an early developing self that he calls the "implicit self." While it is aware of itself, the processes by which it operates are neurobiological-unconscious. They are responsible for the core function of the self—keeping us in regulated states while responding to internal and external objects. It does the primary processing of objects—the automatic, gut responses. I combine this with William James's conceptualization of the self. He defined the self as a system of conscious processes that he called the "duplex self." It is the system by which we process our stream of consciousness. It reflects on the output of Schore's implicit self, i.e. it does a secondary processing of the responses to objects. Schore defined the primary-unconscious system of the self. James defined the secondary-conscious-reflective system of the self. Together, the primary and reflective self systems comprise what Meares, who builds on James's idea, calls the "full self." We'll see that consciousness also has a primary and reflective level. Given that consciousness and self are comprised of the same stuff—implicit and explicit processes—this is not surprising.

In what follows, I argue that states of consciousness and self are organized by affect. It goes like this. Consciousness and self are features of the mind. The mind consists of implicit and explicit processes. They are qualitatively different. They create different states of consciousness that present us with different worlds and dispose us to different ways of being in them. They assemble what the self is conscious of, what functions it can perform, and the subjective experience it has. The mind, along with its features of consciousness and self, is affect state dependent. That is, affect determines whether implicit and/or explicit processes are activated. I begin with a review of affect regulation theory, necessary to understand the influences of affect on consciousness and self.

Notes

1 I draw from Edelman and Damasio for a basic understanding of consciousness and the origin of consciousness in affect. From Damasio, I draw an appreciation of the role on affect and reflective functioning in adaptation.
2 From Fonagy's mentalization theory, I draw for an understanding of bringing affect from an implicit-nonverbal to an explicit-verbal level and the use of the explicit level in reflecting on intersubjective relating and in the exercise of agency.
3 Meares is an expert in John Hughlings Jackson, Pierre Janet, and William James, all of whom figure prominently in what follows. I am also indebted to his understanding of reflective consciousness, for the idea of developing the capacity to process one's stream of conscious and for the appreciation of the centrality of analogous representation in the development of the reflective self.
4 McGilchrist has written the definitive text on the distinctions between right brain implicit and left brain explicit cognition, the different states of consciousness they generate, and the different worlds they present to us.
5 Allan Schore is the father of regulation theory, which provides the understanding of affect and its regulation found here. I have also drawn from him for my understanding the foundational role of the right brain in development, pathogenesis, and therapeutic action, for an understanding of implicit processes, and for the premise of the primacy of affect in mental life.
6 Prior to acquiring consciousness, organisms were responding to objects but had no means of being aware of it.
7 We'll see that affect not only turns the lights on but adjusts them according to the task at hand.
8 He starts about 1.8 billion years ago with clusters of bacteria thriving as multicellular organisms with no central system organizing the whole. The rules for how to maintain life by recognizing and responding adaptively to salient objects are contained in DNA distributed throughout the organism. Instructions were sent chemically. Plants also work this way, without consciousness, bending toward light and sending roots toward water. They are detecting and responding adaptively to objects without any central organizing system such as a brain. If we didn't know better, we would say they have intentions. We know better because having intentions would require that plants were conscious.

   This stage of decentralized instructions was followed by the advent of single-celled organisms called eukaryotic cells, a type of protozoa. They were able to survive independently because they had collected their DNA into a nucleus.

The regulation of the organism was centralized. One can think of the nucleus as the precursor of our brains. Here too the DNA generated chemical instructions dictating responses to objects in support of life. Nutrients, for example, were recognized, taken into the body, processed, and expelled. Note that this was done without a brain or a mind, let alone a conscious mind. "The entire operation," writes Damasio, "is blind and subjectless" (2010, p. 37).

The development of cells with nuclei was followed by the emergence of a new kind of cell—the neuron. It was a game changer. Now instructions about how to respond to objects could be sent both chemically and through *electro*chemical signals. Most importantly, cells were able to change the states of other cells. Networks of neurons would form into a nervous system enabling us to regulate our organs and musculoskeletal system. It would also give rise to what Damasio defines as a mind—processes capable of representing objects and, eventually, of performing mental operations on them.

In the earliest manifestation of the mind, the brain formed circuits capable of representing perceived objects as patterns of neural firings—an unconscious mind. When the brain became complex enough to give birth to consciousness, we became aware of these unconscious representations. We became conscious of our perceptions, conscious of the present. We had "primary consciousness." Now the organism was no longer blind nor subjectless.

9 Damasio uses the term "images" rather than representation. They may be of visual, auditory, physical sensation, etc.

10 Damasio (1999) quips that we should stop blaming Eve for our misery; that it's reflective consciousness that is the culprit.

11 Although he didn't think in these terms, we can now say that he was observing what happened to his patients' states of consciousness when they became dysregulated by a traumatic memory.

12 This is, of course, how Freud and then ego psychologists came to understand the ego—a system of processes that had experiential, observational, and functional aspects (1923). In this regard, the terms "ego" and "self" as I'm defining it are synonymous. This is in keeping with Bettleheim (1984) who argued that "ego" was a mistranslation of "das Ich," which should have been translated as "self."

Bibliography

Bach, S. (1985). *Narcissistic states and the therapeutic process*. New York: Jason Aronson.

Bromberg, P. (1998). *Standing in the spaces: Essays on clinical process, trauma, and dissociation*. Hillsdale, NJ: Analytic Press.

Bromberg, P. (2006). *Awakening the dreamer: Clinical journeys*. Mahwah, NJ: Analytic Press.

Crapara, G., & Mucci, C. (2017). *Unrepressed unconscious, implicit memory, and clinical work*. London: Karnac Books.

Crapara, G., & Ortu, F. (2019). From consciousness to subconsciousness; A Janetian perspective. In G. Crapara, F. Ortu & O. van der Hart (Eds.), *Rediscovering Pierre Janet; trauma, dissociation, and a new context for psychoanalysis*.

Damasio, A. (1994). *Descartes' error: Emotion, reason, and the human brain*. New York: Putnam.

Damasio, A. (1999). *The feeling of what happens: Body and emotion in the making of consciousness*. New York: Harcourt.

Damasio, A. (2010). *Self comes to mind: Constructing the conscious brain*. New York: Pantheon.

Dennett, D. (1991). *Consciousness explained*. Boston, MA: Little Brown and Company.

Edelman, G. (1989). *The remembered present: A biological theory of consciousness*. New York: Basic Books.

Edelman, G. (2004). *Wider than the Sky; the phenomenal gift of consciousness*. New Haven, CT: Yale Books.

Ellenberger, H. F. (1970). *The discovery of the unconscious*. New York: Basic Books.

Emde, R. N. (1983). The prerepresentational self and its affective core. *Psychoanalytic Study of the Child, 38*, 165–192.

Fonagy, P. (2017). Forward. In G. Crapara & C. Mucci (Eds.), *Unrepressed unconscious, implicit memory, and clinical work*. London: Karnac Books.

Fonagy, P., & Allison, A. (2016). Psychic reality and the nature of consciousness. *The International Journal of Psychoanalysis, 97*(1), 5–24.

Fonagy, P., Gergely, G., Jurist, E., & Target, M. (2002). *Affect regulation, mentalization, and the development of the self*. New York: Other Press.

Hartman, H. (1958). *Ego psychology and the problem of adaptation* (D. Rapaport, Trans.). New York: International Universities Press. (Original work published 1939)

Hill, D. (2015). *Affect regulation theory: A clinical model*. New York: Norton.

Hill, D. (2021). Dysregulation and its impact on states of consciousness. In *Interpersonal neurobiology and clinical practice*. New York: Norton.

James, W. (2001). *Psychology; the briefer course*. New York: Dover Publications.

Janet, P. (1901). *The mental state of hysterics*. New York: Putnam.

Maroda, K. J. (2020). Deconstructing enactment. *Psychoanalytic Psychology, 37*, 8–17.

McGilchrist, I. (2009). *The master and his emissary: The divided brain and the making of the Western World*. New Haven, CT: Yale University Press.

Meares, R. (2005). *The metaphor of play: Origin and breakdown of personal being*. New York: Routledge.

Meares, R. (2012a). *A dissociation model of borderline personality disorder*. New York: Norton.

Meares, R. (2012b). *Borderline personality disorder and the conversational model: A clinician's manual*. New York: Norton.

Meares, R. (2016). *The poet's voice in the making of mind*. New York: Routledge.

Nagel, T. (1974). What's it like to be a bat. *The Philosophical Review, 83*(4), 435–450.

Panksepp, J. (2004). *Affective neuroscience: The foundations of human and animal emotions*. New York: Oxford Press.

Panksepp, J. (2012). *The archaeology of mind: Neuroevolutionary origins of human emotions*. New York: Norton.

Ramachandran, V. S. (2004). *A brief tour of consciousness*. New York: Pi Press.

Rapaport, D. (1967). *The collected papers of David Rapaport [1942–1960]* (Merton M. Gill, editor). New York: Basic Books.

Rosengrant, J. (2005). The therapeutic effects of the free-associative state of consciousness. *Psychoanalytic Quarterly, 74*, 737–766.

Schore, A. N. (1994). *Affect regulation and the origin of the self: The neurobiology of emotional development*. New York: Norton.

Schore, A. N. (2003a). *Affect regulation and disorders of the self.* New York: Norton.

Schore, A. N. (2003b). *Affect regulation and the repair of the self.* New York: Norton.

Schore, A. N. (2012). *The science of the art of psychotherapy.* New York: Norton.

Schore, A. N. (2013). Regulation theory and the early assessment of attachment and autistic spectrum disorders: A response to Voran's clinical case. *Journal of Infant, Child & Adolescent Psychotherapy, 12*, 164–189.

Schore, A. N. (2019a). *Right brain psychotherapy.* New York: Norton.

Schore, A. N. (2019b). *The development of the unconscious mind.* New York: Norton.

Searles, J. (2008). The self as a problem in philosophy and neurobiology. In *Philosophy in a new century*. Cambridge: Cambridge University Press.

Shane, E. (2018). A relational self psychological approach to the clinical situation. *Psychoanalytic Dialogues, 28*(6), 687–695.

Solms, M. (2021). *The hidden spring*. New York: Norton.

Tronick, E. (2004). Why is connection with others so critical? The formation of dyadic states of consciousness and the expansion of individuals' states of consciousness. In E. Tronick (Ed.), *The neurobehavioral and social-emotional development of infants and children*. New York: Norton.

Tronick, E., & The Boston Change Process Study Group. (1998). Dyadically expanded states of consciousness and the process of therapeutic change. *Infant Mental Health Journal, 19*(3), 290–299.

Winnicott, D. S. (1971). Transitional objects and transitional phenomena. In *Playing and reality*. London and New York: Routledge.

Chapter 1

The Bottom of the Mind

A basic premise of the proposed model is that consciousness and self are organized by affect. We need first to understand what affect is and how and why it ebbs and flows, explodes and implodes. For those familiar with my previous book (Hill, 2015) which focused on Schore's regulation theory, this chapter will serve as a review and update. Here, I've woven in the work of Antonio Damasio (1994, 1999, 2010) and John Hughlings Jackson's theory of neural dissolution (Franz & Gillett 2011; Jackson, 1931). I've also included a section on the primacy of affect that locates regulation theory in relationship to other psychoanalytic models.

What Is Affect?

Let's begin with the experience of affect. It is the experience of the state of the body. It has two dimensions. *Arousal* refers to the infusion energy into or the withdrawal of energy from the body. The body is being energized or enervated. *Valance* refers to the positive or negative tone of the experience. Stern (2010) notes that affective experiences have "shapes". They may surge or burst, linger or recede abruptly, etc. He understands affect to be our basic life force, our "elan vital."

Most of the time affective experience is a continuous, background flow of aliveness that is preconscious—available to consciousness when we focus our attention on it. Consciousness has only so much bandwidth and must be allocated to what matters at the moment. Affective experience becomes conscious only when it deviates sufficiently from our baseline state to warrant our attention.

Affective experience is what the defenses of dissociation and repression aim to prevent. Ultimately, it's not the content of traumatic memories or disturbing thoughts in general that are defended against. Rather, it is the

DOI: 10.4324/9781003266617-2

anticipated experience of the affect accompanying them. If we can tolerate the affect, we can tolerate the content.

It's also important to understand affect as *the representation of the state of the body*—hyper- or hypo-aroused, positively or negatively valanced. It may be represented at the neural-chemical level, where it is unconscious; at the somatic-*experiential* level, where it is preconscious; and at the cognitive level, where it is conscious. At the neural level, affect is represented by patterns of neural firings. At the experiential level, it is represented by the body changing in response to internal or external objects. At the cognitive level, affect may be represented verbally or nonverbally. That is, I can be aware of an affective experience nonverbally as it's happening, and I can leave it at that, or I can name it, "sad," for example, should I need to process it further or communicate it to someone else. Let's look at all this more closely.

The Bottom-Up Progression of Affect

In life-as-lived, the sequence of affect representation from the brain, neurological representation; to the body, somatic representation; and then to the mind, verbal and nonverbal representation looks like this. A friend, approaching from behind, calls your name. Your body is instantly and automatically in a state of positive hyper-arousal. The recognition of his voice has been processed unconsciously at the neurological level, and, based on prior experience, the body has been primed for positive engagement. This somatic experience, caused by the change in the body, is available to consciousness. At seemingly the same time, but actually a half-second second later, the third stage kicks in and you become conscious that you've heard your friend's voice and are happy to see him. Your body already "knew" this. You probably would have conveyed your pleasure simply through implicit communications of affect that breathe life into your words, an upregulated, positively toned "Hey Fred!" No need to make it explicit by adding "It's good to see you." Indeed, making the implicit explicit, putting it into a sentence and thereby slowing things down, may detract from the spontaneity, immediateness, and joyfulness of the moment. It would have moved away from the experiential and taken things to the verbal level of affect representation. Let's break this down further.

Again, the representation of the state of the body begins at the neurological-unconscious level. It then progresses to the somatic-experiential-preconscious level, and then to the verbal or nonverbal conscious level (see Figure 1.1).

The sequence begins with the detection of a salient object (Fred's voice) by the limbic-autonomic system which is located in the right brain. The detection occurs through neuroception before it has attained consciousness (Porges, 2011).

As this information about the object passes through one of the limbic system's structures called the hippocampus, it is compared with memories of prior encounters with similar objects. Based on these prior experiences (and genetic disposition), a prediction is made as to what will happen next. At this point, instructions are sent to the visceral organs, especially the heart, and to the musculoskeletal system. (They are sent via the HPA axis[1] and the autonomic nervous system.[2]) They prime the body to respond to what has been predicted. The evaluation of and response to the object are still unconscious.

The instructions take the form of electrochemical signals sent through the nervous system and hormones sent through the bloodstream. They may be for hyper- or hypo-arousal. A hyper-aroused response prepares us to actively engage the object. A hypo-aroused response deactivates the body, preparing us to respond passively—to not engage the object. This completes the unconscious processing of affect. It has now primed the body and is represented somatically. It has also established our fundamental relationship to the object—positively or negatived engaged or disengaged.

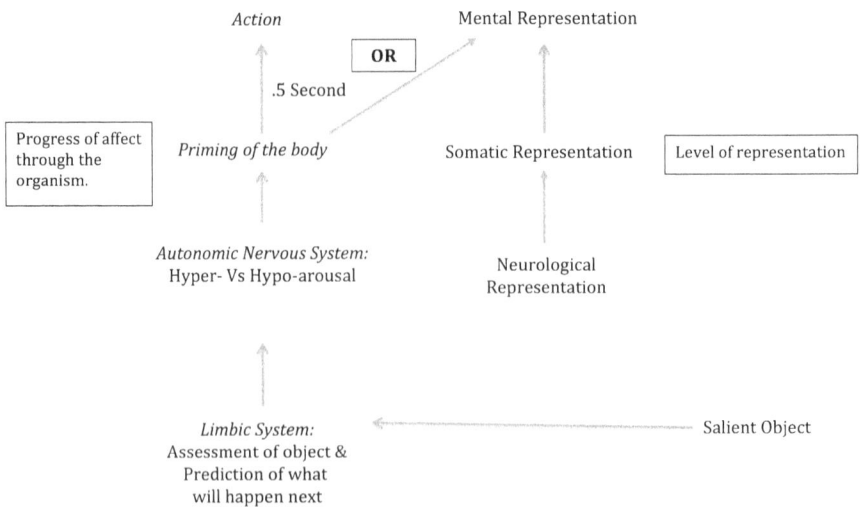

Figure 1.1 Bottom-Up Processing of Affect.

The mid-stage of the process, when the body has changed, is a key moment. Affect has gone through its primary-neurological-unconscious processing and achieved somatic representation. It is now at the preconscious level of awareness and if warranted is available for conscious, secondary processing. The body is now primed for action or inaction, which, *unless we intervene,* is what will happen. However, because affect is available to consciousness, we can intervene.

There is a half a second between the priming of the body and taking an action (Libet, 1981, 1999).[3] Body therapies, such as sensorimotor psychotherapy (Ogden & Fisher, 2014; Ogden et al., 2006) and somatic experiencing (Levine, 1997, 2010), seize this moment to interrupt the process. They focus patients on their bodies to enable them to be aware of the experience and of what's coming next. This is the moment when one can change the scripted response, dictated by the primary processing of affect, to an action of our conscious choosing. Agency is possible.

The verbal-explicit level of affect goes by several names: I'll call it "categorical" affect. Darwin (1872) was the first to study it. He proposed that there were seven categorical affects (fear, anger, joy, surprise, sadness, shame, and disgust). He also saw that each was associated with a specific facial expression and that they were universal.[4] Note that fear, anger, joy, and surprise are supported by hyper-arousal and that sadness, shame, and disgust are supported by hypo-arousal. Hyper- and hypo-arousal, sometimes called "primary affect," are foundational for the higher level, later developing, categorical-verbal affect representations. Also note the greater precision of the explicit affects compared to the simple distinction between positively or negatively toned states of hyper- or hypo-arousal. They enable more differentiated responses to objects. For example, fear and anger are both hyper-aroused and negative, but very different at the categorical level. And they get even more precise. Anger, for example, like other categorical affects, includes a spectrum of intensity extending from annoyed to enraged. Each name/category gives us a better cognitive grasp of the affect and a more precise relationship to the object.[5] *Getting the affect right is crucial for getting the relationship to the object right.*

The Special Place of Implicit-Nonverbal Communication in Psychotherapy

Our bodies communicate. Somatic representations of affect are perceptible to others. We detect them preconsciously in postures, gestures, facial expressions, flushing and blanching of skin, and changes in the prosody of speech (rhythm, pitch, volume, etc.) due to involuntary changes in the larynx (Porges, 2011). Early in development, these implicit communications of affect are the stuff of the "proto-conversations" (Trevarthen, 1979) that occur between infants and mothers.[6] Once we learn to talk, implicit communications from the body stream alongside our words. They are involuntary changes to the state of our body as it responds to objects—our gut reactions. They reveal what objects mean to us, or at least what our scripted, spontaneous reactions to them are.

Regulation theory (Schore, 1994) proposes that implicit communications are at the core of clinical work. They convey information about our spontaneous experience of one another. They mediate the "implicit relationship." They are preconscious. Schore argues that implicit communications are the basis of the therapeutic alliance, that they mediate the transference and countertransference, and that they are at the heart of therapeutic action. We might also say that they mediate the personal relationship or the subject-to-subject relationship. Martin Buber (2023) would say that mediate the "I-Thou" relationship. Winnicott (1960) thought of such spontaneous gestures as expressions of the "true self." For now, my point is that implicit communications convey information about our subjective experience. The person receiving the communication has a spontaneous somatic response to it, which is, in turn, responded to by the other person who has a spontaneous, somatic response to it, and so on. Such ongoing, bidirectional, spontaneous, body-to-body, preconscious exchanges of affect are at the core of intersubjective relating. Trevarthan (1979) called this "primary intersubjectivity." In therapy, we attune to and regulate our patients' affect states with implicit communications. They are responsible for the felt sense of connection we establish with them. They are mediated by the right brain.[7] Schore proposes that implicit communications are at the core of the therapeutic process mediating the implicit therapeutic relationship, and what he calls right-brain-to-right-brain psychotherapy (1994, 2019).

The Neurological Processing of Affect

As we've just seen, one way to think about the processing of affect is its progression from neural, to somatic, to mental. The sequence of the neural processing is also important. Affective information is first processed in the right brain with implicit processes and then in the left brain with explicit processes. Understanding this sequence will ground the discussion of states of consciousness that follows.

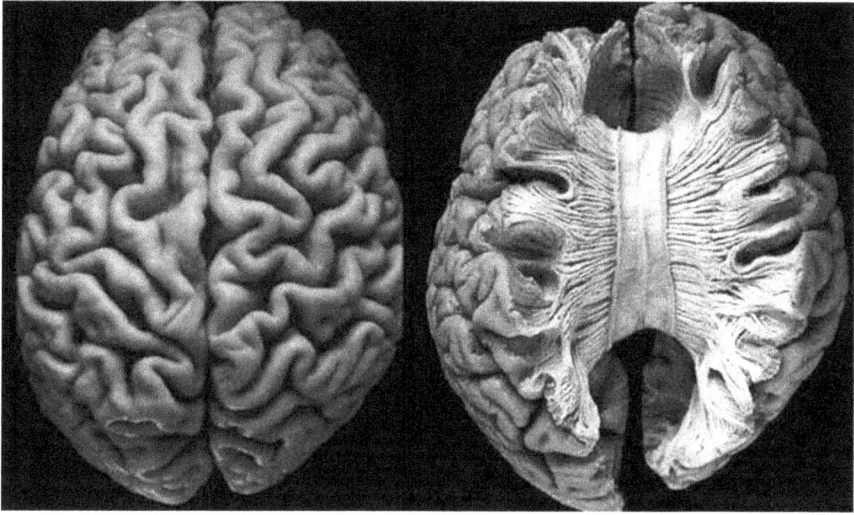

Figure 1.2 A View from Above and Below of the Right and Left Hemispheres. Note the Corpus Callosum Connecting Them.

Our brain is divided into right and left sub-brains (see Figure 1.2). The right brain mediates implicit-unconscious processes. The left brain mediates explicit-conscious processes. The two brains operate independently of one another, serve different functions, and generate starkly different states of consciousness. They are connected by the corpus callosum through which they exchange information (see Figure 1.2).

The neural processing of affect follows a route laid down by the developmental sequence of the brain. The right brain develops first. Its critical period of development is from the third trimester of pregnancy through 18 months. The left brain begins to develop in earnest during the second year.[8] Using unconscious, electrochemical processes as it responds to objects, the right brain does the initial-primary processing of affective information. After being processed unconsciously in the right brain, affective response to the object may be transferred to the left where it receives a secondary, conscious processing using explicit processes—words and sentences. That is, one's primary-involuntary reaction to an object, the product of unconscious processes, may be subjected to a secondary conscious, voluntary processing. Then, after the second take on the response to the object, that information is returned to the right brain where it is integrated with existing memory determining how one will respond to similar objects in the future. The explicit can become implicit.

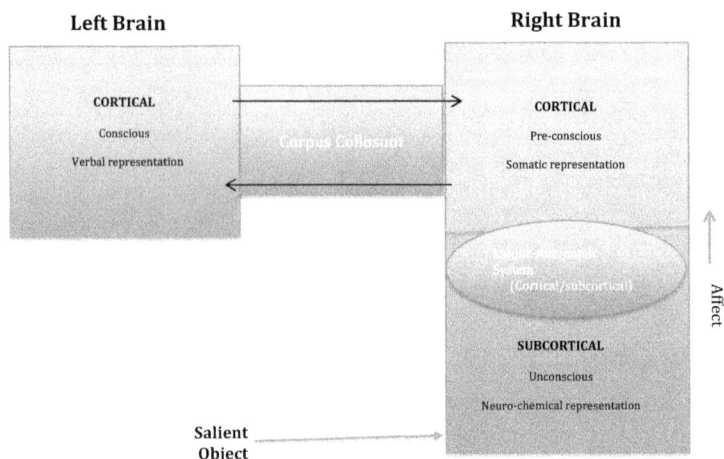

Figure 1.3 Neural Route of Affective Information.

Let's go through this again, but this time with an eye on where it's happening in the brain (see Figure 1.3). It's an updating by Schore (1994) of Freud's topographical model. Recall that affect begins with the detection of a salient object. At this point, affect is represented unconsciously at the neurobiological level. This is the point at which neural and chemical instructions, based on predictions of what will happen next, are sent to the visceral organs and musculoskeletal system. Now the body is primed and our relationship to the object is established. All this processing, measured in milliseconds, occurs subcortically in the right brain.

Affective information then progresses to the cortical level of the right brain where it becomes preconscious. The information then passes across the corpus callosum to the left brain where it becomes conscious and available to secondary, explicit processes that are conscious and voluntary. Affective information then returns across the corpus callosum to the prefrontal cortex of the right brain where it is integrated with memories of similar objects. This is the route affect takes when it is not defended against.

Defenses Against Affect: Repression and Dissociation

Affect may be defended against by dissociation or repression. Dissociation occurs when we become dysregulated or when we anticipate becoming dysregulated. The limbic-autonomic system becomes disorganized (aka disintegrated or disassociated or, most commonly, dissociated[9]). As a result, affect does not complete its primary processing, the information does not make it to the right prefrontal cortex where it would be preconscious where—there is hope for agency, and it is not transferred to the left brain where it would become conscious, available for secondary processing, corrected, and learned from. Rather, the dysregulation generates a dissociated-disordered state of consciousness, an experiential marker of dysregulation-dissociation at the neural level.

Repression, on the other hand, refers to the case in which a highly stressful, negative affect has become conscious. It has completed its primary processing, but let's assume, for example, that the associated events are deemed shameful. We may then defend against it becoming conscious again. This is accomplished by classic ego defenses such as rationalization, denial, disavowal, and intellectualization—all conscious, cognitive, secondary processes mediated by the left brain. Note that the dissociation of affect occurs at the neurological level when the organism *is* dysregulated. It will also occur when dysregulation is anticipated. Repression is accomplished at the psychological level to defend against affect that has become conscious and that we anticipate would dysregulate us were it to become conscious again. While there are costs to repression, it preserves as much adaptive functioning as possible.[10]

Affect Regulation and Dysregulation

The fundamental aim of the brain and the conscious mind it gives rise to is to keep the body alive. Reproduction is important, but the first job of living things is to stay that way. The mind and consciousness evolved because they made us better at it.[11] Normally, staying alive means, first and foremost, keeping the organism in regulated (homeostatic) states and thereby maximizing adaptive responding to objects. What does being regulated or dysregulated actually mean and what does staying regulated involve? How is that related to maximizing adaptive responding? A heuristic called the *windows of tolerance* devised by Pat Ogden helps to explain. I've added categorical affects and some terms we need to define (Figure 1.4).

Again, affect may be hyper- or hypo-aroused. Note that both hyper- and hypo-aroused affect states may be regulated or dysregulated. In regulated states, we function optimally. The structures of the brain are integrated, exchanging information reciprocally. We can process both our body-based

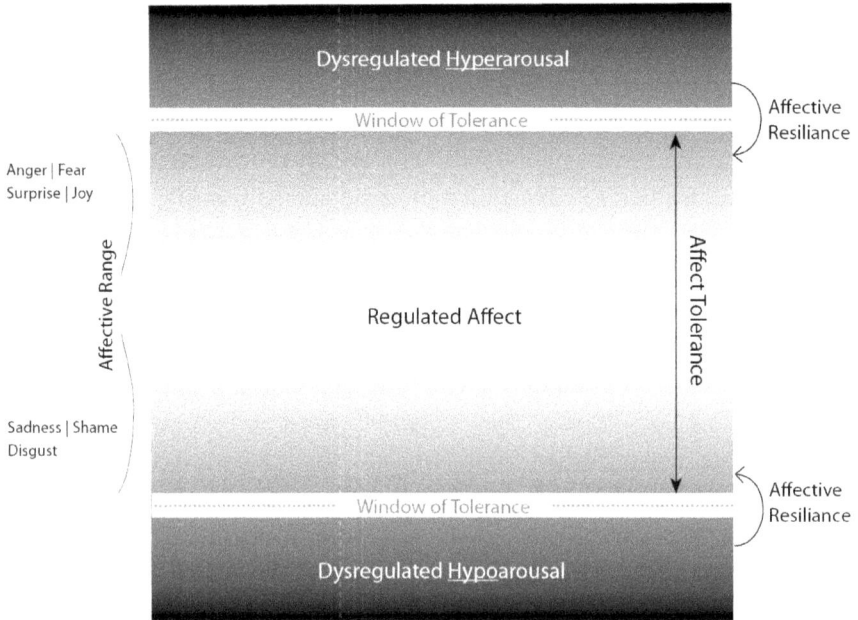

Figure 1.4 Windows of Tolerance.

affect and the socio-emotional affect streaming from others via implicit communications. We are alert, all our cognitive operations are available, and we can focus our attention where needed. We can think coherently and deliberately. We are able to act agentically. We have a sense of self-mastery.

The dysregulated zones represent what happens to the brain and mind, and to functioning and subjective experiencing when we are unable to modulate the intensity of hyper- *or* hypo-arousal. Once we've exceeded our tolerance for either, the brain becomes disorganized-dissociated. As we've just seen, affect is thus dissociated and never moves beyond the unconscious, subcortical, neurochemical level, able to generate actions but not available to consciousness. With the dysregulation-dissociation of the limbic system, we are unable to process our own body-based affect. Subjectivity collapses. Without the capacity to process implicit communications of affect from others, intersubjectivity collapses. On top of this, when we're dysregulated, reflective processes are deactivated. We lose the capacity for higher order, secondary, cognitive processing. We are unable to conjure our inner world and use it to think and act intentionally. We're operating without crucial information and acting automatically without the capacity for agency. We lose all sense of self-mastery. We've all been in such states ranging from being head over heels in love, to marital spats, to losing our resolve and breaking a diet, to lashing out, and to, on the hypo-aroused end, not being able to speak or act, to being deactivated.

Returning to Figure 1.4, let's define some terms.

- The *windows of tolerance* refer to the outer edges of regulation where we're on the verge of either hyper- or hypo-aroused dysregulation.
- *Affect tolerance* is a measure of our capacity to modulate the intensity of affects, thereby keeping them within the boundaries of regulation.
- The distance between the windows of affect regulation also represents our *affective range*. If our regulatory capacities are maldeveloped, we may be restricted to categorical affects supported by only hyper- *or* only hypo-arousal. For example, preoccupied attachment trauma results in a disposition toward hyper-arousal. In that case one will be inclined toward and even restricted to joy, fear, anger and surprise. Avoidant attachment trauma results in a disposition toward hypo-aroused affect states, in which case one will be inclined toward and even restricted to shame, disgust, and sadness.
- We all become dysregulated occasionally and are familiar with the loss of higher order functioning that occurs and the effort required to restore self-regulation. The capacity to return efficiently to regulated states after becoming dysregulated is our *affective resiliency*.

A fundamental goal of affect regulation therapy is to enhance affect tolerance, and resiliency. Mastery of one's affect when stressed preserves the capacity to reflect, to relate intersubjectively, and to act agentically.

Neural Regression

What accounts for the loss of higher order functions when dysregulated? Our understanding of the neurobiological basis of this phenomenon originates in the work of John Hughlings Jackson, the mid-19th-century father of English neuroscience. His ideas influenced an extraordinary array of theorists including Charcot, Breuer, Freud, James, Piaget, Vygotsky, and more recently Damasio, Edelman, Schore, and Meares. He was the first to distinguish right and left brain processes and to observe that the earliest developing form of consciousness is assembled by the right brain. Like many today, he proposed that consciousness is an emergent phenomenon resulting from increases in neural complexity and argued that as the brain increases in complexity, culminating with the development of the prefrontal cortices of the right and left brains, there is an extraordinary increase in the complexity of consciousness. He was the first to conceptualize consciousness as having lower and higher forms (Franz & Gillett, 2011; Janet, 1901; Meares, 2005; Schore, 2003).

Along with his theory of the development of consciousness, Jackson (1931) proposed a theory of "neural dissolution." He argued that "assaults" (stresses) to the brain result in neural disorganization and that the last structures to develop are the first to become disorganized. The development of the right brain precedes that of the left, and subcortical development precedes cortical development.[12] Thus, when stressed there is a loss of cortical and left brain functioning—a loss of reflective processing. We are reduced to primary consciousness. Higher order functioning is incapacitated. The greater the stress, the greater the disruption of neural functioning and thus the greater the degradation of conscious processing. Jackson saw this as a regression down the evolutionary trajectory to a more primitive, earlier developing form of consciousness. Janet (1901) proposed the same idea, in which "vehement emotions" led to a "lowering of consciousness." Jackson's theory of neural dissolution explained the "narrowed" states of consciousness Janet observed in hysterical patients when they encountered traumatic memories.

Summary and conclusion: When affect is regulated the mind is organized. Dysregulated affect disorganizes it. When affect is regulated, our brain is optimally integrated, and we have access to our higher order, reflective processes. When we're dysregulated, the later developing neurobiological systems that subserve reflective consciousness become disorganized-dissociated (Meares, 2012; Schore, 1994; Vaitl et al., 2005). We find ourselves in a lower-constricted state of consciousness with diminished cognitive and affect processing capacity. Our capacity to function adaptively is affect state dependent. This is one of many ways that the primacy of affect is evident in regulation theory.

The Primacy of Affect: The Bottom of the Mind

The primacy of affect is a premise of regulation theory. The idea goes back at least as far as the philosopher David Hume who, in 1736, in *A Treatise of Human Nature,* disputed the accepted notion that our highest aim is to be as rational as possible and rid ourselves of emotional influence.[13] He argued that our goal should be to get emotion right because it determines the direction reason takes.[14] He argued that we don't arrive at our convictions by rational argument. Rather, we argue *from* emotionally based convictions.

Schore begins his seminal text for regulation theory (1994) with the idea that nothing is more important for survival than the regulation of the organism. He goes on to give the regulation of affect primacy for optimal and pathological development and for therapeutic action. Neuroscientists Damasio (1999), Edelman (2004), and infant researcher Daniel Stern (2010) understand consciousness and self to originate in affective experience, in what Damasio calls "the feeling of what happens" as our body changes in response to objects.

We can also see the primacy of affect when Damasio (1994, 1999) argues that affect assigns "adaptive value" to objects, alerting us to opportunities and dangers. Ultimately, affects tell us what matters to us. It directs our attention, determines our aims, and, as Hume argued, recruits our cognitive processes in its service. It fuels and directs our actions. At the level of personality, hyper- and hypo-arousal define such basic fault lines as active-passive, extroverted-introverted, dominant-submissive, assimilating-accommodating, and manic-depressive.

We can also see the primacy of affect in treatment. Implicit communications of affect mediate the transference-countertransference and the therapeutic alliance—the subjective-personal aspects of the relationship. They are the medium by which we attune to and regulate one another, by which we connect, and by which we feel felt. Such mutual exchanges of affect, mediated by implicit communications, are the life blood of the therapeutic process, the primal stuff of psychotherapy.

In pathology, we can observe the primacy of affect in the hyper- versus hypo-aroused types of PTSD, the former of which manifests as hypervigilance and flashbacks, the latter of which manifests as social withdrawal and depersonalization (Lanius et al., 2005, 2006, 2010). Similarly, we see affect primacy in the differences between preoccupied (hyper-aroused) and avoidant (hypo-aroused) attachment patterns (Schore, 1994) and in the inflated and deflated types of narcissistic personality disorder (Bach, 1985, 1994). Recall that hyper-arousal and hypo-arousal are mediated by the autonomic nervous system, which Jackson (1931) called "the physiological bottom of the mind."

The Primacy of Affect and the Psychoanalytic Models

Where does this place regulation theory in relationship to other psycho-analytic models? By the 1970s, psychodynamic clinicians were faced with several competing theories. Integrating them became for some, me included, a holy grail. Pine (1990; see Hill, 1994 for a synopsis) came up with a particularly elegant idea for how to deal with this embarrass-ment of riches, one that I adopted and taught for many years. He pro-posed that each of the major schools of thought, which he considered to be "drive psychology," "ego psychology," "object relations," and "self psychology," depicted a different organization of mind—different "psy-chologies." He further proposed that our minds fluctuate among them and that each of these psychologies was prominent and clinically relevant at different moments when patients were in different states of mind. He then argued that we should apply each of the models as needed. This made perfect sense at the clinical level and is probably the way most of us now practice.

The problem was at the theoretical level. Each school posited an issue of primacy to which all phenomena could be traced. Drive psychology pos-ited the primacy of drives and their regulation by the ego. Ego psychology posited the primacy of the ego which was understood to be involved in both internal adaptation—the regulation of the drives—and external adap-tation to the environment. Object relations theory proposed the primacy of the object. Objects are internalized into patterns of self in relationship to object and different patterns are activated in different circumstances. Self-psychology posited the primacy of the self and the need to maintain a sense of coherence, continuity, and self-esteem. I would add to this list rela-tional psychoanalysis and the primacy of intersubjectivity. Psychoanalysis remained without a unified theory, but Pine's model freed us from having to decide among the competing theories.

Why doesn't regulation theory take its place alongside the other models? They are psychologies.[15] Their focus has been on the mind, and although there is increasing awareness that it is embodied none have successfully integrated this into their theories. Regulation theory is a psychobiology. It is about the *bodymind*. It proposes that the mind emerges out of the body and that, fundamentally, the mind is in the service of the body helping to keep it alive and thriving. It's the body, its state represented by affect and regulated by the limbic-autonomic nervous system, that's primary. The mind, with its features of consciousness and a homunculus, is an add-on.

Psychoanalysis may be changing in this regard. Eagle (2022) notes that ego psychology is a theory of the regulation of the drives, and that it suffers from failing to have a theory of affect. He also notes that Fenichel (1945) argued that all ego defenses are defending against affect. Sandler (1981) writes "A psychoanalytic theory of motivation related to the control of feeling states should, I believe, replace a psychology based on the idea of an instinctual drive discharge" (p. 188; See also Lichtenberg, 1989; Modell, 1993). Kernberg (1975) put affect front and center with his understanding that the fundamental units of mental life are self in an affective relationship to objects. Fonagy and his colleagues (2002) seem to have also taken this position writing that "Mentalized affectivity lies, we suggest, at the core of the psychotherapeutic enterprise. It represents the experiential understanding of one's feelings in a way that extends beyond intellectual understanding." Finally, shortly before his death, I corresponded with Fred Pine asking if I had represented him accurately and if he had any comments. He responded, "I have no argument with your summary of my work, and certainly not to the primacy of affect."

Finally, let me add this. According to regulation theory, the mind is organized from below by the limbic-autonomic system. The most efficient therapeutic change requires therapeutic actions directed toward this foundational system. Such changes derive from new experiences mediated nonverbally by implicit communications of affect. These mediate body-to-body exchanges of affect that establish the implicit therapeutic relationship. The different psychologies depicted by the psychoanalytic models ride on top of this neurobiological, primary affect regulating system. Psychological responses are downstream from changes in the body that have already occurred in response to objects. Of course, both levels of intervention are important. The mind is changeable through cognitive, "top-down" intervention such as observations and interpretations, but the limbic-autonomic system is foundational.

Notes

1 The HPA axis is comprised of the hypothalmus, pituitary, and adrenal glands that distribute hormones and neurotransmitters.
2 The autonomic system has a sympathetic component that regulates hyper-arousal and a parasympathetic component that regulates hypo-arousal. Ideally the system is balanced with the sympathetic and parasympathetic

subsystems offsetting one another. This allows us to shift flexibly and fluidly between hyper- and hypo-aroused affect states.

3 William James (2001) seems to have been the first to realize that physiological change precedes psychological awareness of affect. Levine summed up this "bottom-up" understanding of the processing of affect as "…rather than running because we are afraid, we are afraid because we are running" (2017, p. 129).

4 There is controversy among affect theorists about the number of discrete affects and whether they are universal. In what follows, for the sake of discussion, let's stick with Darwin's seven.

5 For a fuller understanding of the mentalization of affect, see Hill (2015, pp. 105–109) and Jurist (2019).

6 The mother is whoever keeps the infant in regulated states.

7 More specifically, they are mediated by the right temporoparietal junction (Schore, 2019).

8 Throughout the brain, later developing structures are capable of inhibiting those that develop earlier. In this case, the later developing left brain can inhibit the earlier developing right brain where affect receives its primary processing. Said differently, the secondary, explicit processing of the left brain can suppress the implicit, primary processing done by the right. This is seen when patients defend against affect by intellectualizing or rationalizing.

9 The term "dissociation" is used to refer to the breakdown of the reciprocal exchange between neurological or psychological structures that should be exchanging information. Here I'm talking about neurological dissociation, but the term has been applied, confusingly from the point of view proposed here, to the dissociation of self-states (Bromberg, 1998, 2006). "Repressed" or "compartmentalized" self-states would have been preferable.

10 At this point, there are no known neural mechanisms and no generalizable neural correlates for repressive defenses (Holmes, 1990). Dissociation resulting from dysregulation, on the other hand, has been shown to be associated with a distinct imbalance in the limbic-autonomic system and a resulting disorganization-dissociation among its neural structures (Bremmer et al., 2010; Frewen & Lanius, 2015; Vaitl et al., 2005). A corresponding limbic-autonomic imbalance is proposed by Schore (1994). Neural dissociation is also addressed by Meares's (2012) research on P3a,b.

11 Damasio (1994, 1999) argues that consciousness evolved because it allows us to apply thought to the problem of maintaining homeostasis and responding adaptively to objects, and thus better at surviving and thriving.

12 The earlier developing structures serve the autonomic regulation of the organism, whereas the latter developing cortical structures subserve flexible thinking and voluntariness.

13 Hume was refuting Descartes. Supported by neuroscience, Damasio makes a similar argument in *Descarte's Error* (1994).

14 McGilchrist, also refuting Descartes, makes a parallel argument when he proposes that the left hemisphere does the bidding of the right. The right processes

affect first, and based on its evaluation and response to what is predicted of encounters with an object, it enlists the left brain to find meaning in its action, to make it happen, and to rationalize what it wants to do.

15 Drive psychology, which understands the mind to be in the service of the body's urges for sex and aggression, is the exception. At its heart, it is a psycho*biology*, but it was developed as an ego psychology emphasizing the mind and never developed a theory of affect. Contemporary Freudians, it should be noted, are, I believe, attempting to overcome these limitations. Indeed, from what I can tell, all the psychoanalytic schools are attempting to incorporate "embodiment" into their theories.

Bibliography

Bach, S. (1985). *Narcissistic states and the therapeutic process.* New York: Jason Aronson.

Bach, S. (1994). *The language of perversion and the language of love.* Northvale, NJ: Aronson.

Bremmer, J. D., Vermetten, E., & Lanius, R. (2010). Long-lasting effects of childhood abuse on neurobiology. In R. A. Lanius, E. Vermetten, & C. Pain (Eds.), *The impact of early life trauma on health and disease: The hidden epidemic* (pp. 166–177). Cambridge: Cambridge University Press.

Bromberg, P. (1998). *Standing in the spaces.* Hillsdale, NJ: The Analytic Press, Inc.

Bromberg, P. (2006). *Awakening the dreamer: Clinical journeys.* Mahwah, NJ: Analytic Press.

Buber, M. (2023). *I and Thou.* New York: Free Press.

Damasio, A. (1994). *Descartes' error: Emotion, reason, and the human brain.* New York: Putnam.

Damasio, A. (1999). *The feeling of what happens: Body and emotion in the making of consciousness.* New York: Harcourt.

Damasio, A. (2010). *Self comes to mind: Constructing the conscious brain.* New York: Pantheon.

Darwin, C. (1872). *The expression of the emotions in man and animals.* Chicago, IL: University of Chicago Press. (Reprinted in 1965)

Edelman, G. (2004). *Wider than the Sky; the phenomenal gift of consciousness.* New Haven, CT: Yale Books.

Franz, E. A., & Gillett, G. (2011). John Hughlings Jackson's evolutionary neurology: A unifying framework for cognitive neuroscience. *Brain, 134,* 3114–3120.

Frewen, P., & Lanius, R. (2015). *Healing the traumatized self.* New York: Norton.

Hill, D. (1996). Pluralism as a driving force in psychoanalysis. In D. Hill and C. Grande (Eds.), *The British schools of psychoanalysis.* New York: Jason Aronson, Inc.

Hill, D. (2015). *Affect regulation theory: A clinical model.* New York: Norton.

Holmes, D. S. (1990). The evidence for repression: An examination of sixty years of resear. In J. L. Singer (Ed.), *Repression and Dissociation* (pp. 85–102). Chicago: University of Chicago Press.

Jackson, J. H. (1931). *Selected writings of J.H. Jackson. Vols. 1 and 2*. London: Hodder and Soughton.

Janet, P. (1901). *The mental state of hysterics*. New York: Putnam.

Jurist, E. (2019). *Minding emotions: Cultivating mentalization in psychotherapy*. New York: The Guilford Press.

Levine, P. (1997). *Waking the tiger: The innate capacity to transform overwhelming experiences*. Berkeley, CA: North Atlantic Books.

Levine, P. (2010). *In an unspoken voice: How the body releases trauma and restores goodness*. Berkeley, CA: North Atlantic Books.

Levine, P. (2017). Emotion, the body and change. In M. Solomon & D. Siegel *How people change* (pp. 127–150). New York: Norton.

Libet, B. (1981). The experimental evidence of subjective referral of a sensory experience backwards in time. *Philosopy of Science, 48*, 182–197.

Libet, B., Freeman, A., & Sutherland, K. (1999). *The volitional brain: Towards a neuroscience of free will*. Devon: Imprint Academic.

Liotti, G. (1992). Disorganized/disoriented attachment in the etiology of the dissociative disorders. *Dissociation, 5*, 196–204.

Liotti, G. (2004). Trauma, dissociation, and disorganized attachment: Three strands of a single braid. *Psychotherapy: Theory, Research, Practice, Training, 41*, 472–486.

Meares, R. (2005). *The metaphor of play: Origin and breakdown of personal being*. New York: Routledge.

Meares, R. (2012). *A dissociation model of borderline personality disorder*. New York: Norton.

Modell, A. (1993). *The private self*. New York: Harvard University Press.

Ogden, P., & Fisher, J. (2014). *Sensorimotor psychotherapy: Interventions for trauma and attachment*. New York: Norton.

Ogden, P., Minton, K., & Pain, C. (2006). *Trauma and the body: A sensorimotor approach to psychotherapy*. New York: Norton.

Pine, F. (1990). *Drive, ego, object and self*. New York: Basic Books.

Porges, S. (2011). *The polyvagal theory: Neurophysiological foundations of emotions, attachment, communication, and self-regulation*. New York: Norton.

Schore, A. N. (1994). *Affect regulation and the origin of the self: The neurobiology of emotional development*. New York: Norton.

Schore, A. N. (2003). *Affect regulation and disorders of the self*. New York: Norton.

Schore, A. N. (2019). *Right brain psychotherapy*. New York: Norton.

Stern, D. N. (2010). *Forms of vitality*. New York: Oxford University Press.

Trevarthen, C. (1979). Communication and cooperation in early infancy. A description of primary intersubjectivity. In M. M. Bullows (Ed.), *Before speech: The beginning of interpersonal communication* (pp. 321–348). New York: Cambridge University Press.

Vaitl, D., Birbaumer, N., Gruzelier, J., Jamieson, G. A., Kotchoubey, B., Kübler, A., Lehmann, D., Miltner, W. H. R., Ott, U., Pütz, P., Sammer, G., Strauch, I., Strehl,

U., Wackermann, J., & Weiss, T. (2005). Psychobiology of altered states of consciousness. *Psychological Bulletin, 131*(1), 98–127.

Winnicott, D. W. (1960). Ego distortion in terms of true and false self. *In The maturational process and the facilitating environment: Studies in the theory of emotional development* (pp. 140–157). New York: International Universities Press, Inc.

Chapter 2

States of Consciousness

Levels and Styles

My aim in this chapter is to provide a clinical model of consciousness. States of consciousness determine the nature of the world we know and profoundly influence our way of being in it. I argue that they are affect state dependent. I will describe changes to our state of consciousness that occur as our affect state changes in response to internal and external objects. The capacity to shift into the most adaptive state of consciousness for the task at hand is also affect state dependent. Appreciating such changes provides an understanding of our patients' subjective experience and shifting adaptive capacities. Here are the rudiments of the model.

There are two levels of normal waking consciousness: a lower, primary level and a higher, reflective level. Babies are thought to enter the world experiencing the primary level. The reflective level starts to emerge during the second year.[1] The lower level, *primary consciousness*, consists of the simple phenomenological awareness of the surround and of one's existence at the center of it. There is awareness, but no awareness of awareness, no meta-cognition. One is restricted to the present. There is no inner world in which to pull back and reflect. There are not yet higher order processes by which to reflect, and there are no representations of things not present. There are just perceptions of the present. Lizards probably experience primary consciousness. Whether insects do is more in doubt.

Primary consciousness has one level. *Reflective consciousness* has two. Among other things, it reflects on the primary level. Reflective processes operate in a virtual world of mental representations. It allows us to think about things in their absence, and thus to consider the past and the future. We are also in states of reflective consciousness when we observe ourselves in real time.

There are two styles of consciousness. Implicit consciousness is constructed by implicit processes. They are mediated by the right brain.

DOI: 10.4324/9781003266617-3

	Left Brain	Right Brain
Cortical-subcortical	Reflective Explicit Consciousness	Reflective Implicit Consciousness
Subcortical	Primary Explicit Consciousness	Primary Implicit Consciousness

Figure 2.1 States of Consciousness: Levels and Styles.

Explicit consciousness is constructed by explicit processes mediated by the left brain.[2,3] The world we know in implicit states of consciousness is qualitatively different from the one we know in explicit states. The contrast resembles the difference between the lushness and subtlety of impressionist art and the abstraction and starkness of minimalism. Experiencing people as complex subjects like oneself is one among many characteristics of implicit consciousness. Experiencing people as objects of use is one among many characteristics of explicit consciousness. Both styles of consciousness operate at primary and reflective levels. That is, we can be in states of primary or reflective implicit consciousness, and we can be in states of primary or reflective explicit consciousness (see Figure 2.1). This chapter describes these different states of consciousness.

Finally, the model attempts to account for shifts between implicit and explicit, and between primary and reflective states of consciousness. We've seen that affect is constantly changing in response to objects, and that getting the affect right gets the relationship to the object right. We'll now see that getting the affect right also gets the state of consciousness right, i.e. that changes of affect in response to objects induce shifts of states of consciousness that are adaptive for the task at hand.

Levels of Consciousness: Primary and Reflective

As the brain becomes increasingly complex, so do our states of consciousness. Infants come into the world as subcortical right brain creatures equipped with only implicit-nonverbal processes and experiencing only *primary implicit consciousness*. They are limited to the perception of the

Phase of Development	Type of Consciousness	Capability
Infant: subcortical right brain	Primary implicit	Process real-time, themselves in center without past and future
Second year left brain development	Primary explicit	Process real-time with ability to name objects
Prefrontal cortex development (right)	Reflective implicit	Meta-awareness in present allows observation of self interacting with objects in real-time.
Prefrontal cortex development (left)	Reflective explicit (Verbal-reflective)	Verbal reflecting on past and future

Chart developed by Maria Rappaport

Figure 2.2 The Development of Consciousness.

present. Without reflective consciousness, without an inner world in which to time travel, they remain in real time all the time, without past or future. It's a nonverbal existence of continuously changing perceptions infused with affective experience resulting from responses to perceived objects. In the second year, the left brain begins to develop. We see rudimentary expressions of verbal processes[4] and of *primary-explicit consciousness*, for example, an infant who has begun to point at objects and name them. At this point, there is still no inner world with its appraisals of and associations to the object. The object is recognized and has a name. That's it. Primary explicit consciousness is verbal, but there is only one level.

Once the prefrontal cortices of the right and left brains begin their development, a second level of consciousness emerges. *Reflective implicit consciousness* is a nonverbal meta-awareness of what's going on in the present. Once it develops, we are able to observe and assess ourselves interacting with objects in real time. Normally, it operates in the background, alert to danger. When necessary, it operates in the foreground and guides our real-time actions. *Reflective explicit consciousness* is verbal. It operates in our inner and outer worlds (speaking to ourselves and speaking to others). It allows us to think in words about the past and future. I'll refer to it as *verbal-reflective consciousness* (see Figure 2.2).

The importance of the development of reflective consciousness, the doubling of the mind, cannot be overstated. It was responsible for the cognitive revolution mentioned earlier and the modern society to which it led. Closer to home, it supports complex forms of memory (episodic memory, autobiographical memory, and working memory). Prior to the capacity for these complex forms of memory, there was only recognition memory, semantic memory, and implicit-procedural memory. (We'll come back to this.) Reflective consciousness supports agency and enables the self to develop itself. As we'll see, when we're dysregulated this, all collapses; reflective processes are deactivated, and we're reduced to a single-level state of consciousness and non-agentic, scripted acting.

The Primary Levels of Implicit and Explicit States of Consciousness

Levels of consciousness can only be understood in conjunction along with the style with which they occur. Since we have yet to discuss styles, for the sake of discussion, I will temporarily oversimplify them.

Recall that primary consciousness is the simple, phenomenological awareness of the present, a world of perception only in which one is aware of only the surround and of one's existence in it. One is immersed in and pressed up against the present, experiencing a direct, wordless awareness of it.[5] It's mediated subcortically by the right brain. Because it is constructed by implicit processes, it is more fully described as primary implicit consciousness.

We get a sense of *primary implicit consciousness* when we are in-the-moment—immersed in the present. However, normal experiences of being in-the-moment are actually partial immersions in the present. A reflective level of consciousness is operating in the background, monitoring what's going on in real-time and available for full deployment if necessary. Everyday being in-the-moment comes with a background awareness of being able to step out of it, and we normally do dip in and out. We tend to think of being in-the-moment as a positive experience, and it is when it's a voluntary state. This is possible when affect is regulated. Being in-the-moment involuntarily as a result of dysregulation is another matter entirely and produces an unmitigated experience of primary implicit consciousness.

We enter primary implicit consciousness involuntarily during states of severe hyper-aroused dysregulation. Think of an instance in which you've slipped and caught yourself. The survival system is activated. The state of arousal shoots up. Instantly, reflective processes are deactivated. You are simply aware of what's happening and of your automated reactions. Note that primary implicit consciousness doesn't have to be a negative state. Consider again the single-level consciousness of infants before the complexity of the brain has developed sufficiently to support reflective consciousness. Watch them in states of quiet alert, processing what's in front of them, wide-eyed and unblinking, simply taking it all in, seemingly immersed, even mesmerized, and intensely curious, perhaps in a state of wonder.[6] This too is primary implicit consciousness.

Primary explicit consciousness begins as the language centers of the left brain start to come online. As mentioned above, we see this with one-year-old infants who have achieved the capacity for semantic memory (remembering names of things) and begin to point at objects and name them. There is no reflective activity in this. There are no thoughts about or around the object. There is just the word coincident with the object—just one level.

We get a sense of this in cases of patients who talk to us and give the impression that there are no thoughts associated with the words. Rather, they refer matter-of-factly to whatever they are discussing, offering a chronicle of events that seem to be without personal meaning. When they relate an incident to us, they are pointing at themselves taking part in event without thoughts around and about what they're saying. We quickly become bored.

Newirth (2020) offers a vivid description of the experience of being in states of primary explicit consciousness. He references Grotstein (1995) who thought of such individuals as "Orphans of the Real." Newirth writes

> I have often thought of the T.S. Eliot poem, "We are the Hollow Men." as expressing the hopeless, meaningless, unthinking experience of being stuck in a never-ending external world of things as they are. … an unimaginative, thoughtless state of mind…their inability to use reverie and metaphors in developing a personal world inhabited by new subjective meanings, identities, and hopeful relationships.
>
> (p. 81)

Disordered states of consciousness like this may be defensive and momentary, or they may be chronic. In either case, the left brain, mediating explicit processes, is dominant. The later developing left brain inhibits the primary processing of affect by the right brain.[7] Consciousness is devoid of the affect that would give life to the words, connect them to the body, and make them personal. But it's not only flattened affect that makes such patients stressful to work with and difficult to engage. Consciousness is also flattened. There is a cognitive constriction—an absence of thoughts associated with what's being said. Meares (2005) notes that to be in such states of consciousness, without an inner world, is to live on the surface.

We also see such left brain states on the receptive side of verbal process-ing. I asked a patient what he thought about a criticism his wife had of him. She had said that he acts as though he doesn't hear a word she says. He replied, "It's really about her complaining about me all the time." "How so?" I asked. He responded in a resolute tone, "I hear the words." When I asked him to say more about it, he replied with a shrug, "I can repeat them back to her." Another patient, whose mother could become enraged and verbally abusive, described her experience of it with a gesture of helpless-ness as she told me, "It goes in one ear and out the other." Nothing beyond the words themselves is processed as they pass through. In both cases, the affect was dissociated *and* there had been a regression to a constricted, state of single-level, primary explicit consciousness.

The Reflective Levels of Implicit and Explicit States of Consciousness

With the development of the right and then the left prefrontal cortices, con-sciousness acquires a second level. We achieve the capacity to reflect. Recall that there are two types of reflective consciousness. With the development of the prefrontal cortex of the right brain, we acquire the capacity to reflect on the present. This is called *implicit or nonverbal reflective consciousness.* Now we can generate, in real time, a wordless thought, a gestalt depicting and assessing the scene we're in. This capacity to reflect nonverbally in real time allows us to guide our actions as we are acting.

With the development of the prefrontal cortex of the left brain, we acquire the capacity for *verbal-reflective consciousness.* We use it to think in words about the past and the future. We become able to conjure a vir-tual world in which to re-present to ourselves things that we've perceived in the past. We can hold such representations in attention and perform mental operations on them. Equipped with this inner world, we are no longer confined to the present, no longer stimulus bound. We become able to direct our thoughts, recall past events, and imagine future possibilities. We are capable of hindsight. We can plan. Temporal context and delib-eration become a part of consciousness. Mature defenses such as ration-alization and intellectualization develop. Both require an inner world and verbal-reflective processes. Primitive repressive defenses such as avoidance, projection, and splitting operate at the primary level (Salas & Turnbull, 2010).

At some point, we become aware that this inner world is ours and ours alone. Privacy comes into being, marked in children by the arrival of secrecy and lying. With an inner world and its reflective processes, agency becomes possible. We are no longer stimulus-response machines but rather we can intervene and have some say about the matter.

Reflective Processing and the Complexity of Consciousness

Just as the epigenetic development of a second level was a cognitive revolution for the species, the second level makes extraordinary contributions to the complexity of the child's consciousness. Consider the development of one- and two-level memory systems. At first, the infant is equipped with only recognition, semantic, and implicit memory. Recognition memory is the instantaneous remembering of objects. Semantic memory involves remembering the names of objects and facts about the world such as the number of days of the week—the kinds of things we "just know." Implicit memory is the remembering of procedures. These enable us to automatize actions such as those involved in riding a bicycle and interacting with others in real time. No reflective processes are involved in these early forming memory systems. There is just one level.

Later developing memory systems—episodic, autobiographical, and working memory—have two levels. They allow for surprising complexity. For example, in the case of episodic memory, we recall being part of an event. Note the complex structure of the memory. It is of oneself, experienced as "I" in the present, thinking about oneself, experienced as "me" in the past. We experience ourselves simultaneously as a subject, the knower, in the present, and as an object, the known, in the past. In states of primary consciousness, we know ourselves only as a subject. There's only the "I" and no "me"—only one level. In reflective states of consciousness, we can know ourselves as a subject and an object.

There are a variety of reflective processes essential to development and adaptive functioning. Mentalization, the verbal assessment of our own and others' mental states, is a reflective system of particular adaptive importance. However, any kind of analysis requires a doubled consciousness in which we step back from the present and into our inner world where mental operations are applied to mental objects. Talking to ourselves about anything requires two levels.

The jewel in the crown of reflective processing is what William James (2001) and then Russell Meares[8] (2005, 2012a, 2012b, 2016) have focused on—the processing of one's stream of consciousness. Like episodic memory, it has an "I-Me" structure. The experience is that "I" am processing a flow of thoughts and feelings that I experience as mine—indeed as "me." Here again one experiences oneself as both subject and object. The subject, "I," is constant, always experienced as the same person.[9] The object, "me," is always changing. James called the state of consciousness in which one is processing one's stream of consciousness the "duplex self." I will argue in Chapter 3 that this is a system by which the self comes to know and develop itself.

The Influence of Affect on Levels of Consciousness

Finally, how are we to account for involuntary shifts from double- to single-level states of consciousness, from complex to constricted states. The key lies in whether affect is regulated or dysregulated. In regulated affect states, we shift between levels flexibly and automatically as the situation warrants. Consider your own experience in a good conversation with a friend in which you find yourself moving into the moment, toward a single level of consciousness, and then you step back from the moment and into your inner world to reflect. Back and forth between degrees of immersion in and detachment from the present. Our state of consciousness adjusts from moment to moment to the task at hand.

In dysregulated states, we are reduced involuntarily to single-level states of consciousness. Depending on the degree of dysregulation, reflective capacities are impaired or deactivated entirely. In severely dysregulated states of hyper-arousal, such as fight or flight, we lose reflective capacity completely. We regress involuntarily to a primary level of implicit consciousness, limited to an awareness of the present and reduced to automated functioning. Only recognition and implicit memory systems are operational. Think again of slipping. You are instantly in state if primary consciousness. Note that experience is limited to an awareness of the surround and of your automated reactions (procedures). In states of dysregulated states of hypo-arousal, we are reduced to states of primary explicit consciousness. (We'll come back to this issue of states of consciousness being determined by hyper- versus hypo-arousal in the next section.). Such regression to a less complex state is in keeping with Jackson's principle of neural dissolution. When affect is dysregulated, later developing-higher-order-cortical-reflective processes are deactivated. We become scripted, operating with subcortical processes and experiencing primary consciousness.

Let me now turn our attention from levels to styles of consciousness. As I warned, I've included a few aspects of implicit and explicit styles into the above discussion of levels. There is, however, a great deal more to appreciate about their workings beyond verbal versus nonverbal, and the processing of the present versus the past and future, and much more to consider about the different ways that implicit and explicit processes construct the world we know and how we are disposed to be in it.

Styles of Consciousness: Implicit and Explicit

While levels of consciousness determine whether we have an inner world in which to reflect, styles refer to different ways of thinking and different things thought about. We'll see that the way our right and left brains know things, and the kinds of things they know are so different that they present us with very different worlds and dispose us to different ways of being in them. Optimally, either way is available to us as the situation demands (Tweedy, 2020a). Like levels, styles of consciousness shift so they are suitable to the task at hand, and like levels, styles of consciousness are affect state dependent. However, in the case of styles, the issue isn't whether affect is regulated or dysregulated, but rather whether it's hyper-aroused or moderately aroused.

Implicit Versus Explicit States of Consciousness

The left and right brains mediate different processes that generate different states of consciousness. The left brain mediates explicit processes. They operate at the verbal level and produce sentences and narratives in which information is presented serially, one piece at a time. They are linear and logical. They serve to communicate thoughts to others. They are also used to break down complex ideas into parts and subject them to analysis. They are conscious and we can direct them. They process the past and the future. They are too slow to process the present.

The right brain mediates *implicit processes*. They operate at the neurological level. They are automatic, ultra rapid, and unconscious. They process the present. There is a suite of them. We've discussed the implicit communication of affect. We've also encountered implicit-procedural memory. There is also implicit learning, learning without realizing you're learning, and there is implicit cognition. It is basic to implicit consciousness.

Implicit cognitions are the result of the right brain's capacity to synthesize information. The results come to us as gestalts—nonverbal, fully formed thoughts in which, like visual images, all the information is presented simultaneously. For example, if I asked you who the first person you spoke with this morning and what was said, the episode would come to you first as a gestalt, the nonverbal whole of it presented to you in one fell swoop. It arrives as an image of some sort, not necessarily visual although often described as thinking in pictures. We also saw a gestalt in the example I gave of real-time reflection. We can produce a snapshot and assessment of the scene we're in, all the information presented simultaneously.

Implicit cognition coordinates with explicit cognition. Imagine a discussion in which an opinion pops into mind. It's a complex thought that presents itself as a whole. You can sense that you know implicitly what it's all about and can come up with the reasoning supporting it. The form of gestalts like this opinion of yours is difficult to pin down. They are imagistic, a thought-cloud that somehow it contains the seeds of everything you will need to know to explain it. William James (2001) described it as a "diffuse" experience accompanied by a "feeling of knowing" what's in it.

If you launch into unpacking your opinion and explaining it to another person, you have begun to employ your left brain. You are now using explicit processes that break the gestalt into its parts and convey verbally, in a stepwise linear fashion, piece by piece, logically and according to syntactical rules, whatever it was that went into your opinion. Out of the diffuse gestalt, you wind up with a series of precise, propositional sentences like this one that can be strung together into a coherent narrative.

We saw this sequence of the right brain, implicit cognition followed by the left brain, explicit cognition in Hume's idea that we argue *from* our emotionally based convictions. We also see it in our everyday clinical life. As Hume would have predicted, most of our interventions begin, not as the result of a methodical buildup of conscious reasoning, but rather with a complex thought assembled unconsciously.[10] Like the opinion, this intuitive understanding comes to mind all at once and is followed by a figuring out of what went into the idea.

Such clinical intuitions derive in part from *implicit learning* that we have been accumulating without realizing it. Patterns have been recognized and information organized without awareness of having done so. As we tell the patient whatever it is that we've intuited, we're simultaneously monitoring ourselves using *implicit-real-time reflection*. Here it acts as a hovering awareness that guides us in the present, alerting us with a reassuring feeling when we're expressing what we want to say with reasonable accuracy and sensitivity, and an uncomfortable feeling when we're not getting it right enough.

Implicit processing may be most fully appreciated in the functioning of the infant during the first 18 months of life. Especially at first, it's a purely implicit creature. It's noteworthy that the "mother"[11] is the most complex object to which the infant must adapt, yet the implicit processes of the right brain alone are responsible for attaching to her. Their relationship is mediated by *implicit communications of affect* by which they read one another's internal states. With repetition, these interactions are encoded as *implicit-procedural memories* that will script their "relational moves" and contain their *implicit expectancies*. Measured in microseconds, they become their automated ways of being with their mothers and then with others. (Beebe & Lachman, 2002; Lyons-Ruth, 2000). Along with these behaviors, the baby is developing what the Boston Change Process Study group called "implicit relational knowing" (Lyons-Ruth et al., 1998)—a specialized type of implicit cognition that guides their relating.

Note the kind of object that implicit processes are specialized to assess and respond to. The object is an alive thing, a subject with an internal state that is continuously changing as it responds to objects. Detectable changes take place in microseconds and can be extremely subtle. Despite the complexity of this problem, the assessing and responding to the state of the subject happens in real time, the result of implicit processing.

Such alive, continuously changing, unique objects are qualitatively different from the static, abstracted objects without inner states that are known to the left brain. Whereas the right brain detects and assesses subjects like us, we'll see below that the left brain detects and assesses objects of use. The right brain subjectifies, whereas the left objectifies.[12] Meares (2005, 2012) notes that Jackson wrote about what he called subject and object consciousness being generated by the right and left brains. More recently, Bach (1985) has drawn attention to subject and object awareness (aka subject and object consciousness, respectively), which has had considerable influence on our understanding of self-reflexivity (Aron, 2000) and therapeutic action (Rosegrant, 2005). We'll come back to this in Chapter 3.

We are, of course, familiar with the conscious, deliberate, explicit processes of the left brain that were used to unpack your opinion. They are verbal, linear, and conform to the rules of narrative. They are specialized not only for unravelling and explaining our thoughts to others, as we saw with the opinion, but also for analyzing how things work and for mastering and using them. We'll see in Chapter 3 that they are also used for exploration and in the service of self-development.

Let me take a moment to gather and elaborate a bit on what we've covered to this point. There are several varieties of implicit-unconscious processes. *Implicit communications* are of most immediate interest clinically. They are somatic expressions of affect. Our body speaks through facial expressions, the shaping of sounds as we speak, and our posture and movements. They are spontaneous expressions of our subjective experience and the means by which we read one another's internal states. From the first moment of meeting one another, we are detecting and adjusting to one another's affect states (Schore & Schore, 2008). Without conscious effort, we *implicitly learn* one another's set points, affect patterns, and tolerances, which will inform our *implicit relational knowings* about how to interact.

Implicit communications of affect are at the core of clinical process— preconscious communications that mediate transferences, countertransferences, the therapeutic alliance, and therapeutic actions (Schore, 1994). Importantly, it is these exchanges of affect—split second matching, recognizing, resonating, and responding to one another's affect states — that give us the felt sense of a connection with one another. *Implicit memories* store procedures learned through repetition. The procedures become hardwired and script our behaviors. We rely on them for automatized activities. Finally, the right brain also mediates *implicit cognitions*. They take the form of gestalts that are presented to us fully formed. They are full of information that we sense is there and that we can make explicit.

The richness of implicit cognition versus the efficacy of explicit cognition: It's important to appreciate the richness and depth of the affectively infused gestalts served up by the right brain, compared with the sparseness and shallowness, *and* usefulness of the left brain's affectless, linear, verbal cognition. We see this in the case where a person is assessed as an object of use rather than a subject. Compare the thinness of such objectifying processes with the depth of thought that goes into appreciating others in their full subjective complexity.

Here's another example of the expanse and complexity of implicit cognition. Recall the example of me asking you who was the first person you spoke with this morning and what was talked about. You were presented with an episodic memory, a gestalt. Let's assume that you had run into a problematic neighbor with whom you have a "polite" relationship. In telling me of this encounter, it would take paragraphs to convey all the thoughts you had, and imagined he had, during the various moments of the encounter. Yet with the arrival of that memory, you sensed all of this implicitly—the wonders of diffuse, nonverbal representation.

Although William James didn't use the terms "implicit" and "explicit," he writes about these different kinds of knowing in a chapter of his *Brief Course of Psychology* (2001) entitled "The Stream of Consciousness." I have found no better understanding of implicit thought. He compares its depth, complexity, and dominance in mental life with the bare bone quality of explicit thought. James, the father of American psychology, was arguing against empirical philosophers, the psychologists of his time. They were attempting to understand consciousness by breaking it down into its parts and building to the whole (reductionism). He proposed the opposite and argued for the use of introspection as the method of inquiry. He wanted to begin with the experienced, directly known, whole of consciousness. His observations led him to argue for the "...reinstatement of the vague and inarticulate to its proper place in mental life..." (p. 164). He believed that the most significant aspects of mental life are not found in bounded representations, such as words, but in the nonverbal knowing that surrounds them. He provides us with the metaphor of a stream to depict the experience of consciousness.[13]

...the definite images of traditional psychology form but the very smallest part of our minds as they actually live. The traditional psychology talks like one who should say a river consists of nothing but pailsful, spoonsful, quart potsful, barrelsful, and other molded forms of water. Even were the pails and the pots all actually standing in the stream, still between them the free water would continue to flow. It is just this free water of consciousness that psychologists resolutely overlook. Every definite image in the mind is steeped and dyed in the free water that flows around it. With it goes the sense of its relations near and remote, the dying echo of whence it came to us, the dawning sense of whither it is to lead. The significance, the value, of the image is all in this halo or penumbra that surrounds and escorts it,—or rather that is fused into one with it.

(p. 164)

What is now understood as implicit knowing, James called the "halo of relations around the image." This halo of *relations* provides an implicit awareness of context. For James, "…knowledge about a thing is knowledge of such relations," a knowledge of associations and implications that are known implicitly. The pots and pails in the stream of consciousness are like words—explicit representations in which meaning is categorized and sharply defined. The implicit knowledge radiating from the words, James's "free water of consciousness," makes up most of the stream. It is known nonverbally. It is the stuff of implicit consciousness.

We see implicit consciousness at the micro level in Daniel Stern's (2004) understanding of the "present moment." He proposes that we experience the present in "chunks" that range from one to several seconds. Each chunk of the present encompasses an awareness of what just happened, what is happening, and what we expect to happen immediately after. Take any moment, for example, a moment in your high school cafeteria in which you nod hello to someone while you are in the midst of a conversation with someone else—and you'll find that the present, constructed by the right brain, is a flow of such micro-gestalts. When unpacked, each moment is found to be highly complex, full of "implicit knowings." In the case of the nod, there are thoughts surrounding the recognition of the person you nod to, and perhaps thoughts about their relationship to the person you're speaking with, and the implications of that if any, and on and on. Stern notes that each present moment is a "world in a grain of sand."

Finally, a mundane example: We can appreciate the richness, speed, and pervasiveness of implicit knowing in the everyday phenomenon of knowing what someone is going to say before they say it. Consider how much we must know about what's going on at that moment and about one another to pull this off. And we compute it in real time. Occasionally, we may interrupt the person with whom we're speaking to interject a response to what we know they are about to say. They accept this implicitly when we've gotten it right or correct us when we're off. Complex overlays of implicit communications are batted about and mutually understood implicitly, all in the midst of communicating explicitly. This orb of knowing is James's "free water of consciousness."

I'm glad to have a left brain, but, left to its own devices, it would sacrifice an extraordinary amount of awareness for the sake of the clarity, precision, and efficacy offered by explicit cognition. Of course, much of the loss would be due to the lack of emotional information processed by the right brain, but the limitations of explicit cognition are an important additional factor contributing to the diminished richness of experience when the left brain is dominant.

The consciousness generated by the left hemisphere's linear and logical processes is convergent. It is the product of a closed system that takes in only what can be assimilated into its unyielding systems of logical thought. It is unable to account for the messiness of life, for the ineffable, or for paradox. It is trapped in the logic of "either/or." It suffers from certainty. Recall that the job of the right brain is to take in the perceived world in its entirety and as it is, contradictions, ambiguities, and all. The left brain assimilates information into the schemas by which it operates. By themselves, the words with which the left brain thinks would confine our awareness to circumscribed categories that lack the sphere of knowing that surrounds them. While lacking the tidiness and power of the verbal left, the right brain knows far greater complexity and is capable of divergent thinking.

The processes of the left brain are effective for proving, explaining, or making use of what one already knows. And it has defensive uses. Staying within the straight and narrow confines of explicit thought can serve to repress whatever we don't want to know. Recall my patient who could repeat his wife's words by rote, but not experience their meaning. When dominating defensively, the left brain avoids the pull of the free water where the relationships with objects reside.

Implicit cognitions have no such constraints. The right brain takes in the world as it is. It generates open states that support contradictions, anomalies, and ambiguities. It's unedited. Whereas the logic of the left brain is reductionist, generates certainty, and arrives at single solutions, the right brain generates plausible ideas and accepts uncertainty. It tolerates paradox allowing us to experience transitional objects as real and not real, to love and hate the same person, and to experience ourselves and others as both subjects and objects.

One more thing about implicit cognition. Recall the neural route taken as affect is processed (see Figure 1.3). The affective response to an object begins subcortically in the right brain, where it receives its primary-unconscious processing—our initial, gut reactions. This information then crosses the corpus collosum into the left brain where it can be subjected to a secondary, conscious, verbal-reflective analysis. Finally, the results of the analysis cross the corpus collosum back to the right frontal cortex. Here it receives a final integration with what one already knows. The resulting gestalts are the highpoint of our socio-emotional intelligence. They are our most complex thinking about others and about our relationship to them. When activated, they come to us as implicit relational knowings.

To summarize what we've learned thus far about implicit cognition: Examples include opinions, intuitions, episodic memories, a micro version seen in present moments, knowing what someone is about to say, real-time snapshots of what's happening at the moment, and implicit relational knowings. Each of these nonverbal mentations is presented to us as a gestalt that has been synthesized unconsciously in the right brain. Such wordless, diffuse thoughts, presented to us fully assembled and jammed packed with implicit knowing, are the coin of implicit consciousness. It stands in stark contrast to the explicit, powerfully useful, but constricted consciousness generated by the left brain.

Appreciation of implicit versus explicit consciousness is furthered by understanding the role of attention in fashioning consciousness. The importance of attention has been underappreciated in psychoanalysis. There are two types: global and focal.

Attention: the leading edge of consciousness: We can deepen our understanding of implicit and explicit consciousness by contrasting the experience generated by global attention, mediated by the right brain, with that of focal attention, mediated by the left. Attention is the leading edge of consciousness. We are only conscious of what we pay attention to. The kind of attention we employ sets the stage for the kind of world we know, the kind of objects in it, and how we relate to them. Let me explain.

Global attention is like the diffuse light of a lantern illuminating the whole of a space. Focal attention is like the beam of a flashlight that puts a concentrated light on a part of the whole. It's worth pausing for a moment to experience this firsthand. There are qualitative differences in the experience. Try this exercise. It will provide the direct experience that James argued is the only way to study consciousness.

Stop reading for a moment and take in the whole of the room you're in *without moving your head,* i.e. take in the gestalt. It helps to sit back for this. Spend some time experiencing the state of consciousness it produces.

That done, let me highlight some aspects of the experience. As you settled into global attention, you perceived the totality of the objects in the room. Note that there is an implicit awareness of the relationship of the objects to one another and to yourself. You experience yourself as part of, and not separate from the whole. I am particularly struck by how this way of taking in the world parallels Freud's description of how to listen. "It consists simply in not directing one's notice to anything in particular and in maintaining the same evenly suspended attention…" (1912, p. 111). Freud listened with global attention, with his right brain (Tweedy, 2020b).[14] It's a receptive, open state.

As you returned to reading and using focal attention, the context of all that's in the room disappeared—almost. Alert to the possibility of danger, we continuously monitor the surround.[15] We shift between focal and global attention at the rate of 50–100 milliseconds, well below what we can be conscious of. When we focus our attention on an object, the surround becomes background.

Take in the whole of the room again. Note that the objects perceived by global attention lack the clarity and definition attained through focused attention. Their edges are blurry, more like impressionism than classic realism with its outlined objects. Note also that your attention doesn't rest on any one object but moves about. The objects in the gestalt lack the stability of those we focus on. Left brain-mediated focal attention has a fixedness that allows explicit processes to perform mental operations on mental objects. On the other hand, the gestalt gets the big picture. As mentioned above, awareness of the relationships between objects allows for an implicit knowing of the implications of what's going on—exactly what is needed to navigate the socio-emotional environment. Finally, note that the gestalt created by global attention has depth. We see into the room as we can see into the gestalts of intuitions and insights.

Focused attention, on the other hand, selects each object in isolation. Like the child demonstrating its newfound left brain talents by pointing to and naming things, and unlike the experience being part of the whole generated by global attention, focal attention sets up a sharp distinction between oneself and the selected object. The parts are precisely delineated and fixed, ideal for cognitively grasping and manipulating them, figuring out how they work, mastering and making use of them. Indeed, activating focal attention disposes one toward an instrumental relationship with objects of use. The right brain didn't evolve to make use of things or to get things done. Rather, it performs the preliminary job of employing global attention to take in the whole as it is, to detect salient objects, note their implications, and assess their adaptive value. *Then* the left brain goes into action.[16]

No less importantly, by taking in the whole, global attention supports the recognition of patterns. This includes patterns of faces, sounds, and movements which communicate affect. Through this capacity to read affect states, the right brain detects subjects in states of being that it recognizes as like its own. It provides the intersubjective intelligence that allows us to empathize, cooperate, and compete.[17] Recognizing like-patterns, resemblances, is key.

The linear, verbal processes of the left brain organize the world into reason and narrative and rely on coherence for assessing truth. The measure of truth for the right brain is the correspondence of patterns.[18] Recognizing similar patterns requires holding multiple objects in mind simultaneously. The right brain's capacity to do this allows it to process metaphors in which the pattern of one object is similar to another. Such thinking is lost on the left brain. Its thinking is linear, and objects are processed one at a time. Metaphors come to mind fully formed. The right brain "gets" them all at once. The left brain has to figure them out. The right brain has insights. The left brain analyzes.

Finally, there is this about global versus focal attention. Whereas we relax into receptive states and sit back wide-eyed to take-it-all-in, focusing attention requires deliberateness. It has an effortful, assertiveness-aggressiveness to it. We squint and lean into concentrating on parts. The "male gaze" uses focal attention to highlight parts and their use. It is adaptive for grasping and mastering things in order to make things happen. And finally, the singling out of parts sets us apart and disposes us toward exclusion and competition (Hecht, 2014). In contrast, global attention creates an experience of oneself as part of a whole consisting of subjects like us. It disposes us toward affiliation and nurturance.

Implicit and explicit states of consciousness must be balanced (Tweedy, 2020a). They are assembled by different cognitive processes; generate different, often antagonistic ways of thinking; and incline us toward incompatible ways of being. We must be flexible in their use. Here are some of the worlds we inhabit and ultimately have to reconcile:

- perceptual worlds in which we are immersed in direct experience versus virtual worlds of abstracted experience
- worlds of subjects like us versus worlds of useful objects
- worlds that we are part of and in which objects are experienced in relationship to ourselves and one another versus worlds of isolated objects from which we stand apart
- Implicit worlds comprised of free-floating water versus explicit worlds of pailsful of water—a world of flow versus one thing after another.

These contrasting worlds and ways of being in them are products of the right versus left brain. What accounts for the activation of one brain and its reality, rather than the other? Why at some moments are we in one world rather than the other, and why do some personalities live more in one, sometimes to the exclusion of the other?[19]

The Activation of Implicit Consciousness Versus Explicit Consciousness Is Governed by Arousal

Supported by a wealth of neuroscience, Schore (2012, 2015) has argued that the right brain is activated in states of hyper-arousal and the left brain is activated in states of moderate arousal. It follows that in states of hyper-arousal, right brain-generated implicit consciousness prevails, and in states of moderate arousal, left brain-generated explicit consciousness prevails. We can see this in the immersion in the present, a product of the right brain, versus detachment from the present, a product of the left brain. In states of hyper-arousal, we become immersed in the present, actively engaging with perceptual objects. In other moments, when our level of arousal drops, the left brain dominates. We draw back from immediate experience and reflect on it. Now we are in a virtual world of mental representations. When regulated, arousal ebbs and flows in response to objects, and we shift flexibly and fluidly between being in-the-moment and being removed from it.

Consider, for example, a conversation with a dear friend from college. It has put both of you in good moods—positive states of moderate hyper-arousal that incline you toward engagement and activates the right brain which generates the experience of being in-the-moment. The conversation has arrived at a negotiation of when to eat. You prefer earlier. He prefers later. It's an old, well-worn conflict that turns up reliably at such moments. The good mood has set the stage for a game you've played since you were in school together; a competition of who can best rationalize their personal preference. Rationalizations that walk the line between plausible and absurd get extra points. Speed is of the essence. You lose points for delays. The score is somehow kept between the two of you and the winner is declared by consensus, although there have been contested outcomes over the years. There is no explicit announcement that the game is beginning.

Once it's game-on hyper-arousal puts you both in-the-moment. The right brain, processing the present, is dominant. It's grappling with real-time competition. It's also supporting a transitional state (Winnicott, 1971), a play state in which things are and are not what they explicitly are, and in which who wins matters, but it doesn't. With each back and forth, you are hoping that your next rationalization comes to you.

The game requires a mixture of right and left brain processes. The activation of the right brain allows for the speed of it all, supplies the ideas, and does the real-time reading of my own and my friend's minds. In coordination with this, each time you offer your next rationalization, the left brain is activated. Such moments, in which you pull back into your inner world and activate your left brain to think in words, requires lowering the state of arousal and slowing down. This kind of self-mastery, marked by a fluid alteration between implicit and explicit states of consciousness, can only occur in regulated states. They allow us to find the right balance[20] between our right and left brains and the states of consciousness they assemble.

Dysregulated states are a very different story. There is an incapacity to switch states and thus the loss of hemispheric balance. One finds oneself stuck in a disordered state of either implicit or explicit consciousness depending on whether the dysregulated affect is hyper- or hypo-aroused. We see this most starkly in the two different types of PTSD (Lanius et al., 2006, 2010). When triggered, one is marked by extreme hyper-arousal, right brain dominance, and flashbacks. The other is marked by extreme hypoarousal, left brain dominance, and depersonalization. In the hyper-aroused, flashback type, one becomes immersed in the experience of a traumatic memory to a degree where it is taken for reality. One is reduced to a state of right brain-mediated primary implicit consciousness, without reflective capacities and without the objectifying processes mediated by the left brain. In the hypo-aroused type of PTSD, one is reduced to a state of left brain-mediated explicit consciousness in which one experiences oneself as an object, detached from affective-somatic experience and outside of one's body.

We've all experienced states of consciousness driven by dysregulated hyper-arousal. We saw it above when we looked at the experience of slipping. There I emphasized that one's state of consciousness was reduced to a single level, and that one is involuntarily and fully immersed in the present. Let's revisit slipping, this time with an emphasis on style, on the implicit state of consciousness in which we find ourselves. Here's an example from my own experience.

On a snowy day in NYC, I slipped and caught myself while walking down to the subway. The next thing I knew it was over. I re-regulated, pulled myself together, and went about my commute. I was in the midst of writing this chapter, so I tried to reconstruct the experience. It was encompassed all in one moment, an awareness of the entire scene with me at the center. There was a fellow commuter walking up the stairs who was startled and reflexively put out his arm. I really didn't have a clear image of his arm, just a sense of it. I was simultaneously aware of reflexively grabbing a railing. I also had an awareness of a woman on the stairs in front of me and a flash of concern that I would fall into her. I was simultaneously aware of what had just happened, of what was happening, and of what I feared happening—an example of Stern's "present moment," a gestalt constructed by the right brain.

It was a full-blown state of primary implicit consciousness, a present moment that took in the whole and knew it all simultaneously. The objects were vague, experienced in relationship to one another, and I was in the midst of it all. I don't think there was any reflective processing. The salient objects stood out: the man's arm, the sensorimotor experience of grabbing the railing, and the woman in front of me. I had experienced a neural regression and was processing the moment subcortically in the right brain.

It's not only dysregulated fear states that generate such states of primary implicit consciousness. Think of moments of dysregulated surprise, joy, or anger. Think of any impulsive act. Any dysregulated hyper-aroused affect reduces consciousness to a single level and reduces us to automaticity. It activates global attention and sweeps us into the direct experience of the moment.

Immersion in such states of dysregulated hyper-arousal is at the other end of a spectrum from the detachment generated by states of dysregulated hypo-arousal (Hill, 2015, 2021). Recall again the experience of the patient who processed only the words of his wife's criticisms without any thoughts or feeling about them. As was typical for him when stressed, he had become hypo-aroused and entered a detached state of primary explicit consciousness.

Summary and Conclusion

In this section, I have been discussing states of implicit and explicit consciousness. The starkly different states of consciousness generated by the left and right brains. They create different worlds and dispose us and equip us with different ways of being in them. In the previous section, I discussed levels of consciousness, primary and reflective. When affect is regulated, we shift between primary and reflective states of implicit and explicit conscious according to the task at hand, as our affect states shift in response to objects. When affect is dysregulated, we become stuck in one state of consciousness or the other with impeded or deactivated reflective capacities.

How is all this clinically useful? For the therapist, appreciating the differences between primary and reflective states of implicit and explicit consciousnesses provides a portal into patients' subjective experience at a given moment. Familiarity with the variations in states of consciousness and how they are influenced by affect states sensitizes us to their fluctuations and allows us to make clinical moves accordingly. For the patient, understanding what happens to the conscious mind when one is dysregulated supports mentalization of their experience, crucial for top-down self-regulation, and helpful in reducing shame about such dysregulated moments. I explore this more fully when I discuss disordered states of consciousness in Chapter 4.

Notes

1 Edelman (2004) calls the two levels of consciousness "primary" and "secondary." Damasio (1999) calls them "core" and "extended." Meares (2005) uses, among the other terms, "single" and "doubled." I will refer to them as "primary consciousness" and "reflective consciousness" because of the latter's importance and to be consistent with psychoanalytic theory.

2 Although the processes performing the functions I'll be describing involve networks that have connections to structures throughout the brain, the focal areas of the networks are lateralized. For the sake of ease, I'll speak in terms of the left or right brain as the location of the processes and of states that are right or left brain dominant.

3 Studies of stroke victims and of epileptic patients whose corpus callosum had been surgically severed (called split brain patients), animal studies, and research using experimental techniques such as anesthetizing-deactivating one hemisphere are finding that some functions typically become organized in one hemisphere or the other. This is understood to have adaptive advantages. Such "laterality studies" have confirmed that our two brains have evolved to accomplish very different kinds of tasks by employing different ways of processing information. The differences are so complete that they operate independently from one another reciprocally exchanging information via the corpus collosum.

 After a period of falling out of favor, the appreciation of laterality studies returned as the adaptive advantages of having two such different brains were increasingly understood and as the implications of the findings were elaborated. Daniel Kahneman won the 2002 Nobel Prize in economics for his work in decision-making. Before him it was assumed that economic decisions were made rationally. Michael Gazzaninga, often called the father of cognitive science, upended consciousness studies and won the 2015 William James Fellow Award for lifetime achievement for showing the functional lateralization of the brain. Iain McGilchrist applied laterality studies to states of consciousness, art history, and social criticism. In the clinical realm, Allan Schore, Philip Bromberg, and Russell Meares have been in the forefront. Schore applied them to psychological development, psychopathology and psychotherapy, and the development and functioning of what he calls the "implicit-self." Bromberg devised a relational model and then discovered it was explained at the psychobiological level by Schore's regulation theory. Meares applies laterality studies to his work on therapeutic action and the development of the self.

4 Receptive and expressive centers of speech (Wernicke and Broca areas) are both located in the left brain.

5 Recall also that this primary level of implicit consciousness is a product of the subcortical, implicit processes mediated by the right brain. It synthesizes perceptions as they stream in and presents us with the present.

6 Even after the left brain develops, the right brain dominates mental life until 7–8 years of age which Selma Fraiberg (1959) called the "magic years."

7 Recall that later developing neural structures are capable of inhibiting earlier developed structures.

8 Meares is an expert in John Hughlings Jackson, Pierre Janet, and William James, all of whom figure prominently in what follows. I am also indebted to his understanding of reflective consciousness, for the idea of developing the capacity to process one's stream of conscious, and for the appreciation of the centrality of analogous representation in the development of the reflective self.

9 Damasio, Edelman, and Schore all attribute such constancy to the self's immediate link to the body. Schore (1994) goes further saying that the sense of constancy is due to the recognition one's emotional patterns.

10 See Marx-Tarlow (2012, 2021) for a deep appreciation of the use of intuition in psychotherapy.

11 By "mother," I mean whoever keeps the baby in regulated states.

12 This is of central importance to the understanding of self-reflectivity—the capacity to experience oneself and others as both subjects and objects (Aron, 2000; Auerbach & Blatt, 1996; Bach, 1985). As Aron argues, we learn self-reflexivity implicitly through the experience of participating in relationships that shift roles between being a subject and object. From the point of view of regulation theory, the capacity to be aware of ourselves and others as both subjects and objects requires that we can shift between a state of consciousness dominated by the subjectifying right brain and a state of consciousness dominated by the objectifying left brain. Such switching requires that we are in a regulated state.

13 James's use of metaphor is an example of the richness of implicit cognition. Consider all of the knowing that is packed into the image of a stream.

14 Throughout his writings, Allan Schore notes the similarities between Freud's understanding of the unconscious and the workings of the right brain. We've now seen that implicit processes are unconscious, that we communicate unconsciously with implicit communications, that implicit representations consist of *condensed* knowing's from which meanings extend, that global attention generates an oceanic experience, and that listening for implicit content requires free-floating attention.

15 The example frequently used is that of a bird that must focus on a seed to pick it up and eat it but, using global attention, must also monitor the environment for danger. We use focal attention for prey and global attention to guard against becoming prey.

16 Based on this initial assessment, the left, instrumental brain goes about the job of acting on the findings of the right, emotional brain. This secondary relationship of the left brain to the right is what leads McGilchrist to call his masterwork on the right and left hemispheres *The Master and His Emissary* (2009). The findings of the right, emotional brain tells the left, instrumental brain what to do. This is at the heart of Hume's proposal that we begin with emotionally based convictions and then apply reason to support it.

17 See Aron (2000) for the developmental achievement of having an awareness of self and others as both subjects and objects. He calls it "self-reflexivity." The lack of self-reflexivity may be due to a hemispheric dissociation and dominance of the left brain.

18 Interestingly, Hanly (1990) argued that psychoanalytic schools of thought are distinguished according to whether they rely on coherence or correspondence for getting to truth.

19 Consider, for example, the difference between patients suffering from the cumulative trauma of preoccupied attachment resulting in a sympathetic bias and disposing them to right brain-dominant, implicit states of consciousness, and patients suffering from avoidant trauma and a parasympathetic bias who are disposed to left brain-dominant, explicit states of consciousness.

20 See Tweedy (2021b) for an in-depth discussion of the relationship between the right and left hemispheres.

Bibliography

Aron, L. (2000). Self-reflexivity and the therapeutic action of psychoanalysis. *Psychoanalytic Psychology, 17*(4), 667–689.

Bach, S. (1985). *Narcissistic states and the therapeutic process.* New York: Jason Aronson.

Beebe, B., & Lachman, F. (2002). *The origins of attachment: Infant research and adult treatment.* New York: Routledge.

Benjamin, J. (1990). An outline of intersubjectivity: The development of recognition. *Psychoanalytic. Psychology, 7*(Supplement), 33–46.

Damasio, A. (1999). *The feeling of what happens: Body and emotion in the making of consciousness.* New York: Harcourt.

Edelman, G. (2004). *Wider than the Sky; the phenomenal gift of consciousness.* New Haven, CT: Yale Books.

Fraiburg, S. (1959). *The magic years: Understanding and handling the problems of early childhood.* New York: Scribner.

Freud, S. (1912). Recommendations to physicians practising psycho-analysis. *The Standard Edition of the Complete Psychological Works of Sigmund Freud* 12: 109–120.

Freud, S. (1923). The ego and the Id. In J. Strachey (Ed.), *Standard edition of the complete psychological works of Sigmund Freud* (Vol. 19, p. 111). London: Hogarth Press.

Grotstein, J. (1995). Orphans of the "Real". II: The future of object relations theory in the treatment of psychoses and other primitive mental disorders. *Bulletin of the Menninger Clinic, 59*, 312–332.

Hanly, C. (1990). The concept of truth in psychoanalysis. *International Journal of Psychoanalysis, 71*, 375–383.

Hecht, D. (2014). Cerebral lateralization of pro- and anti-social tendencies. *Experimental Neurobiology, 1*, 1–27.

Hill, D. (2015). *Affect regulation theory: A clinical model.* New York: Norton.

Hill, D. (2021). Dysregulation and its impact on states of consciousness. In *Interpersonal neurobiology and clinical practice* (pp. 169–194). New York: Norton.

James, W. (2001). *Psychology: The briefer course.* New York: Dover Publications.

Lanius, R. A., Bluhm, R., Lanius, U., & Pain, C. (2006). A review of neuroimaging studies in PTSD: Heterogeneity of response to symptom provocation. *Journal of Psychiatric Research, 40*, 709–729.

Lanius, R.A., Vermetten, E., Loewenstein, R.J., Brand, B., Schmahl, C., Bremner, J.D., & Spiegel, D. (2010). Emotion modulation in PTSD: Clinical and neurobiological evidence for a dissociative subtype. *American Journal of Psychiatry, 167*, 640–647.

Lyons-Ruth, K. (2000). "I sense that you sense that I sense...": Sander's recognition process and the specificity of relational moves in the psychotherapeutic setting. *Infant Mental Health Journal, 21*(1–2), 85–98.

Lyons-Ruth, K., Bruschweiler-Stern, N., Harrison, A. M., Nahum, J. P., Sander, L., Stern, D. N., & Tronick E. Z. (1998). Implicit relational knowing: Its role in development and psychoanalytic treatment. *Infant Mental Health Journal, 19*, 282–289.

Marx-Tarlow, T. (2012). Clinical intuition in psychotherapy: The neurobiology of embodied response. New York: Norton.

Marx-Tarlow, T. (2021). Birds of a Feather: The importance of interpersonal synchrony in psychotherapy. In S. Siegel, A. Schore & L. Cosolino, Interpersonal neurobiology and clinical practice (pp. 169–194). New York: Norton.

Meares, R. (2005). *The metaphor of play: Origin and breakdown of personal being.* New York: Routledge.

Meares, R. (2012a). *A dissociation model of borderline personality disorder.* New York: Norton.

Meares, R. (2012b). *Borderline personality disorder and the conversational model: A clinician's manual.* New York: Norton.

Meares, R. (2016). *The poet's voice in the making of mind.* New York: Routledge.

McGilchrist, I. (2009). *The master and his Emissary: The divided brain and the making of the western world.* New Haven, CT: Yale University Press.

Newirth, J. (2021). The generative unconscious and the capacity to be fully alive. In *Vitalization in psychoanalysis: Perspectives on being and becoming* (pp. 82–100). New York: Routledge Press.

Rosengrant, J. (2005). The therapeutic effects of the free-associative state of consciousness. *Psychoanalytic Quarterly, 74*, 737–766.

Salas, C., & Turnbull, O. (2010). In self-defense: Disruptions in the sense of self, lateralization, and primitive defenses. *Neuropsychoanalysis, 12*(2), 172–182.

Schore, A. N. (1994). *Affect regulation and the origin of the self: The neurobiology of emotional development.* New York: Norton.

Schore, A. N. (2012). *The science of the art of psychotherapy.* New York: Norton.

Schore, A. N. (2015). Book Review of *The Emotional Life of Your Brain*, by Richard J. Davidson and Sharon Begley. *Psychoanalytic Psychology, 32*(3), 539–547.

Schore, J. R., & Schore, A. N. (2008). Modern attachment theory: The central role of affect regulation in development and treatment. *Clinical Social Work Journal, 36*, 9–20.

Tweedy, R. (Ed.). (2020a). *The divided therapist hemispheric difference and contemporary psychotherapy.* New York: Routledge Press.

Tweedy, R. (2020b). Introduction. In *The divided therapist hemispheric difference and contemporary psychotherapy* (pp. 1–69). New York: Routledge Press.

Winnicott, D. S. (1971). Transitional objects and transitional phenomena. In *Playing and reality* (pp. 1–34). London and New York: Routledge.

Chapter 3

The Core Self

For a general understanding of the self, I have adopted a widely accepted model of a core-private-inner-personal self and a social-public self. The outer self includes an array of social adaptations—versions of our self that, like the clothes we wear, are appropriate to the situation we're in, to the role we've assumed, and to the way we wish others to think of us. The core self is us in the raw. It's formed by experiences in the early attachment relationship—secure or insecure. Our social selves are developed in the world beyond the mother. The core self is constant, whereas the social self is varied. The state of the self at any given moment is made up of the core self and a version of the social self, ideally with the former guiding the latter. "Self-states" are characteristic configurations of the core self and social self. They make up an array of sub-personalities[1] that have varying degrees of integration with one another (Bromberg, 1998, 2006). Our concern here, however, is not with personality.

This chapter is about the core self. For the sake of readability, I'll refer to it simply as the self. Like consciousness, it originates in and is organized by affect[2] (Damasio, 2010; Edelman, 2004; Schore, 1994). And like consciousness, the self operates at primary and reflective levels utilizing implicit and explicit processes. How could it be otherwise? Recall that consciousness and self are two sides of the same coin—a coin consisting of implicit and explicit processes. When these processes assemble what we are aware of, we call it consciousness. When they perform functions or generate subjective experience, we call it the self.

The Primary (Implicit) Self: Allan Schore has formulated a neurobiological and clinical understanding of what he calls the "implicit self." It

DOI: 10.4324/9781003266617-4

operates with implicit processes. Like implicit consciousness, it has a primary and a reflective level. For the moment, I am concerned with only the primary level. To keep with the scheme I've established, I'll also refer to it as the "primary self," the lower level of the "reflective self." The implicit processes by which it operates are mediated subcortically by the limbic-autonomic system located in the right brain.

It performs the foundational function of the organism—keeping it regulated while responding to objects. All other functions depend on it. It continuously scans the internal and external environments for salient objects and chooses a response to it based on its history with similar objects. When the object is a subject with an inner state, the implicit self processes, in real time, our own body-based affect and the affect states of others, the latter expressed implicitly by their face, prosody of voice, posture, and gestures.

We've been doing this since early infancy. The infant is a purely implicit creature. It knows only the present, communicates only with implicit communications, and exists in an implicit state of consciousness. Schore's regulation theory proposes the centrality of the implicit self in development, psychopathology, and therapeutic change (1994, 2003, 2009, 2010, 2011, 2017). In this model, it is understood as the primary level of core self.

The implicit self is also the experiencing self. By processing affect, it links our mind to the experience of the body providing us with phenomena ranging from the felt sense of affect to the sense of embodiment. Affect attunement is mediated by implicit communications between implicit selves. The synchronization of affect states generates a resonance providing a felt sense of connection and a felt sense of being recognized. It is also the primary-implicit-experiential self that is impinged upon or dismissed—that experiences itself as vulnerable. And it is the implicit self, the self in the raw, that is exposed in the transference and in enactments. It's the primary level of Winnicott's spontaneous, "true self" (1960).

The Reflective Self: Beginning in the second through the sixth year of age, with the development of the prefrontal cortices, a reflective capacity emerges. Now the self has two levels: a primary level and a reflective level that processes the output of the primary level. Two reflective self systems of clinical relevance have been conceptualized.

Mentalization theory describes a verbal-reflective system tasked with the assessment of one's own and other's mental states. Fonagy and his collaborators theorize its development, its failure to develop, and its therapeutic development (Allen & Fonagy, 2006; Allen et al., 2008; Fonagy et al.,

2002). We've already seen that the mentalizing system is responsible for the secondary regulation of affect. In what follows, we'll see its secondary role in intersubjective relating and agentic functioning.

Russell Meares (2005, 2012a, 2016) has also elaborated a reflective system of central clinical importance.[3] He builds on what William James's (2001) called the "duplex self"—the system by which we reflect on our stream of consciousness. Like mentalization, this system goes through a development in the attachment relationship or fails to. I will propose that the processing of one's stream of consciousness is the reflective level of the implicit self and that, among other things, it serves the function of self-generation.

The Self as Experiencer and Doer

In this section, I discuss the self as the locus and maker of subjective experience, and as the performer of functions. Regarding the former, I argue that affect establishes what objects mean to us personally by grounding meaning experientially in the body. As to the functions the self serves, I have delineated four of central clinical interest: the regulation of affect, intersubjective relating, agentic functioning, and self-generation.

The Self as the Locus and Maker of Subjective Experience

Of course, many different factors contribute to subjective experience. In Chapter 2, we saw how our experience of the world and ourselves in it varies according to whether the right or left brain has been dominant in constructing consciousness. We also saw that the level of consciousness contributes to subjective experience. With the emergence of reflective consciousness, we acquire a temporal perspective. Reflective processes also make agency possible, which comes with an experience of self-mastery and a sense of responsibility. And, of course, subjective experience is also influenced by historical, economic, social, and cultural factors. Here, however, I am concerned with the influence of affect on subjective experience through its role in making meaning.

Affect tells us what matters—*personally*. As we detect, assess and respond to salient objects, the positive or negative valence of the affect designates the object's value. The intensity of the arousal, the strength of the affect, indicates the degree of the object's importance. This is first known to us somatically.

The response of *my* body to the object makes it clear, in no uncertain terms, that whatever the object means, it means it to *me*. It is this linkage of the body to the object that is severed by the dissociation of affect. Without the experience of the body responding to objects, we become detached from them or never connect in the first place. They become meaningless to us.

Along with its other responsibilities, generating these fundamental aspects of subjective meaning is the work of the limbic-autonomic system. It is the neurobiological substrate of the implicit self. It first establishes meaning unconsciously at the neurological level. The value given to the object by the affective response to it is based on prior experiences with it that have been encoded as implicit memories. When the object is detected, they are activated and produce our initial, automatic, gut response to the object: hyper- or hypo-aroused and positively or negatively valanced. The primary level meaning of the object to us is established.

Reflective processes play a secondary role in the influence of affect on meaning. Mentalization theory has clarified this. Recall that affect ascends from the unconscious-neurological level to the preconscious-sensorimotor-experiential-implicit level, and then to the conscious level where it can be named. Once somatic experience has been given a name (fear, joy, shame, etc.), verbal-reflective processing allows us to adjust the affect. Take, for example, a case of overreaction in which the gut reaction to the object is overly intense, let's say "furious." If, upon reflection, we determine that "annoyed" is more appropriate, we may be able to lower the affective intensity. Words give us a cognitive grasp of the affect helping us to regulate its intensity from the top down. Down regulating the affect from "furious" to "annoyed" refines and makes more accurate the meaning of the object to us.

The Self as Performer of Functions

Let's shift now from the self as the maker and locus of subjective experience to the self that executes functions. I describe four essential to adaptation: affect regulation, intersubjective relating, agentic acting, and self-generation. Each function has a primary and reflective system.

Affect Regulation: Primary and Reflective Systems

You are already familiar with the primary and reflective affect regulating systems. Here I'll simply provide a brief summary. Recall that the initial-primary regulation of affect is performed by the limbic-autonomic system. It is continuously assessing, unconsciously, via "neuroception," the internal and external environments; detecting salient objects; responding with positively or negatively toned hyper- or hypo-arousal; and thereby establishing our fundamental relationship to the object—engage or disengage, approach or avoid. At the same time, it is modulating the intensity of the affect so that it does not exceed our regulatory boundaries. After this primary-neurobiological-unconscious processing of affect, the mentalization system performs a secondary-verbal-reflective-conscious processing. We just saw this in the case where the verbal grasp of "furious" supported its adjustment to "annoyed." This is a top-down, cognitive regulation of affect as opposed to the bottom-up regulation by the primary system.

Let me stop here with this thumbnail sketch of the primary and secondary affect regulating systems. In what follows, we'll see that the implicit aspect of the self-system performs the primary processing not only of affect regulation but also of intersubjective relating and agentic acting. Likewise, the reflective aspect of the self does the secondary processing of these functions. I don't include the self-generative function because it by definition is a reflective system and, as we'll see, requires the coordinated functioning of the primary and reflective aspects of the self

Intersubjective Relating: Primary and Secondary Systems

Writing from the vantage of self-psychology, Stolorow and his colleagues (Stolorow et al., 1987) introduced the term "intersubjectivity" to psychoanalysis. Shortly thereafter the relational school formed and developed a theory that brought it into mainstream psychoanalytic thinking (Bass, 2019; Kuchuck, 2020).[4] It found empirical confirmation in mother-infant research[5] and established intersubjectivity as an essential function of the self.

Based in Benjamin's theory of recognition (1988, 1990), Aron (1991) defined intersubjectivity as the capacity to appreciate others as separate centers of subjective experience. Benjamin (1990) deepened the idea by appreciating that the capacity for intersubjectivity is a developmental achievement. She reinterpreted Mahler's rapprochement phase not only as the acquisition of object constancy and autonomy but also as a struggle for "recognition" of one's subjectivity. She argued that mutual recognition is at the heart of intersubjective relating, and that intersubjectivity stood alongside the intrapsychic as an independent dimension of psychic life. We'll now see that the implicit system is responsible for primary, nonverbal, real-time recognition, and that the mentalizing system is responsible for secondary, verbal-reflective recognition. Let's start with implicit intersubjective relating. Trevarthan called it "primary intersubjectivity" (1993).

The Primary Intersubjective System: the Importance of Affect Attunement: Recall that, along with the continuous assessment of body-based affect, the limbic-autonomic system is processing implicit communications streaming from others in order to assess their affect states. Given that subjective experience is organized by and around affect, we can say that the limbic-autonomic system is doing the primary processing of our own and other's subjective experience. This primary intersubjective communication system begins to operate during the second month of life.[6]

The primary affect regulating and intersubjective systems are deeply intertwined (Schore, 1994, 2021). They are both performed by the limbic-autonomic system. They develop together. It looks like this. The infant is heavily dependent on dyadic regulation for maintaining self-regulation. Dyadic regulation requires that the mother and the infant detect and respond to one another's affect states. The mother uses the implicit communication system to assess and then up- or downregulate the infant—interactive regulation. The mother is changing her affect states contingently in response to the infant's affect states with the aim of maintaining its self-regulation. Repeated experiences of such interactive regulation become internalized, i.e. they become encoded as implicit memories that script the automated processes of the primary affect regulating system. In this way, the affect regulating and intersubjective capacities of the early attachment figures are transmitted to the infant (Schore, 1994). A two-person process becomes a one-person process.

Through these experiences, the infant is not only internalizing the mother's capacity to regulate affect and engage others intersubjectively, it is also adapting to her ways of engaging. With repetition, "relational-moves," measured in fractions of seconds, are also encoded as implicit memories. These procedural memories support "implicit relational knowing" about how to be together (Beebe & Lachman, 2002; Lyons-Ruth et al., 1998).[7] Thus, as the infant is developing its capacity to regulate affect automatically, it is also developing automated relational moves used in dyadic regulation and intersubjective relating in general. The primary system for processing affect states and the primary system of relational moves combine to form the primary system of intersubjective relating. *Affect attunement* is at the core of the system. How so?

Shore (1994, 2019, 2021) integrates mother-infant research and interpersonal neurobiology to argue, along with Stern (1985), for the centrality of affect attunement in the intersubjective process. He defines affect attunement as the synchronization of affect-states—the simultaneous experiencing of the same affect.[8] This refers to moments such as shared laughter or distress, as well as the less intense, ongoing intermittent attunement that goes on during any intimate conversation, be it verbal or nonverbal (Hill, 2015). As we all know, most dramatically from being in audiences, the synchronization of positive or negative affect states amplifies and prolongs the experience, and generates a mutually felt resonance (Schore, 2019a). In dyads, both parties experience a psychobiological felt sense that it's happening and that the other is having a similar experience.

Although it often operates in the background, the felt resonance resulting from the simultaneous experiencing of affects is a key marker of real-time reciprocal intersubjective relating. Both members of the dyad know implicitly that the other is matching its experience. Moment to moment, they each know what it's like be the other and they each feel known. It creates a sense of "usness" without loss of individuality (Meares, 2005). In treatment, when we attune to our patients, they have a felt sense of being recognized and, importantly, experience a positively toned upregulation.

Sharing the same affect also generates similar states of consciousness (Tronick, 1998, 2004). In dyads, attuned affect states generate a shared state of bodymind that is the fullest expression of intersubjectivity. Intersubjectivists believe that such shared mother-infant experiences are the origin of intersubjective capacity; that they are known by the infant experientially-implicitly; that, over time, they become aware that others have experiences like theirs; and that they too are subjects.

Clinically, affect attunement has powerful therapeutic effects. It generates nurturance in the therapist and provides core affective information for intuitive understanding, empathic relating, and interactive regulation. In the patient, it generates a sense of being recognized and trust. Moreover, affect attunement generates a positive state of hyper-arousal that offsets negative experience and fuels further exploration (Schore, 2012, 2019a).

The Secondary Intersubjective System: We've seen that the mentalization system serves as a secondary system for the regulation of affect. It also serves as the secondary system for intersubjective relating. Mentalization theory demonstrates how the advent of verbal-reflective processes allows the explicit assessment of our own and of others' mental states. It is the secondary means by which we develop an awareness that others have mental states that may be similar or different from our own. Note that when seeking connection, the infant, equipped only with the primary intersubjective system, thrives on matched states and is disrupted by different states. The secondary system is infinitely more sophisticated and is employed to figure out what goes into the difference. Of course, this verbal-reflective system is too slow for real-time interacting. Its analysis of mental states is retrospective or prospective. It provides a reflective, secondary processing of intersubjectivity.

Importantly, a well-functioning mentalization system is not a given, but rather a developmental accomplishment. Its initial development occurs from 2 to 6 years. At this point, the infant has already become implicitly aware of its own and other's affect states. As the prefrontal cortices and the language centers in the left brain come online, infants begin to develop a verbal-reflective system that will be able to do a secondary assessment of their own and other's mental states. The mother begins to make verbal references to affect states, to their motivational aspect, and to what's going on psychologically and why. Over time, the mother teaches the child a "theory of mind" (Rakoczy, 2022) that understands people as agents and behavior in terms of underlying intentions. Such mind-talk involves not only the naming of affects and their gradations but also the verbalization of thoughts about feelings, and feelings about thoughts, and feelings about feelings. One's own and other's mental states can now be analyzed, elaborated, and refined. This is the outcome of a secure attachment relationship. Insecure relationships result in a lack of development or maldevelopment of the mentalization system.

Note that, whereas the operations of the primary system are established by *experiences* in the regulatory relationship encoded as implicit memories, the mentalization system is learned through *talking about minds* with the attachment figures.[9] The system continues to develop throughout the lifespan. Importantly, over time, explicit understandings of mental states may become implicit, known intuitively, and available for use in real-time interactions. Also note that with the development of reflective capacities something new is added to subjectivity. The self acquires the capacity to think and act deliberately, and to direct its actions toward intended goals. Once such agency becomes a known possibility, intersubjective relating becomes a matter of recognizing not only that others have subjective experience but that, also like oneself, they are agents with intentions.

Agentic Functioning: Primary and Reflective Systems

Although there is consensus that agency is a fundamental component of personality development and that, like intersubjectivity, it is crucial for cooperation and competition, and although it is a goal of all psychotherapies, its meaning in the psychoanalytic literature has gone largely undefined and clinically unsystematized. Addressing this issue, Caston (2011) proposes clinical markers for agency: the presence of "self-observation" (reflective processes), "reversibility" (the capacity to choose whether or not to act and to be able to change course at will), and "appropriateness," which I understand to mean directing one's actions toward adaptive goals. Fonagy has rectified the lack of attention devoted to agency with his notion of an "agentic self," a self with the capacity to represent and be aware of its intentions, and to direct its actions toward intended outcomes (Fonagy et al., 2002, 2003).

Classically, the question of agency revolved around whether or not one is acting out repressed wishes with the illusion of agency. However, for Caston and Fonagy, and in what follows, agency is understood as the capacity to direct one's actions toward intended goals in real time. In this case, there can be no illusion about whether one is or is not acting agentically.[10] Consider, for example, that real-time agency usually goes unnoticed. However, when agency is retained under stress, one becomes aware of it and experiences a sense of efficacy and well-being (Modell, 1985), and perhaps a measure of pride. When stressed to the point of dysregulation, the loss of agency is accompanied by fear, and often shame about what's being revealed and/or about having lost control over one's actions.

So, the hallmark of agency is the capacity to act intentionally (Bandura, 2018; Fonagy et al., 2002), i.e. to have awareness of what one intends to have happen and mastery over acting toward that end. Actions include those of the mind and body. Mastery of the mind involves the capacity to direct one's attention and thoughts in desired directions. Mastery over what one does with one's body includes whether one speaks or not, and whether one has command over what one says and how one says it. We can say that agency is distinguished by volitional thinking and acting, but that is not the whole of it.

I include among agentic actions the capacity to loosen control and allow actions of the mind and body to flow spontaneously such as occurs when playing, when speaking freely, and when improvising a relationship in real time. Spontaneous acts are agentic in the sense that, unlike impulsive acts, we can inhibit them if we wish. They differ from deliberate acts in that, while they are voluntary, they are not premeditated. We simply allow them. Thus, agentic actions may be either deliberate or spontaneous.

We must be regulated to be agentic. When dysregulated, we are automated—involuntarily activated or deactivated. The right brain is disorganized. As a result, the affect driving the action/inaction is not receiving primary processing and thus is dissociated and can't be processed reflectively. Moreover, as we've seen, due to neural regression, higher order, reflective processes are deactivated. Without access to the dissociated affect and without reflective capacities to guide us, we enact whatever the primary processing of affect dictates. This automated response will be based on responses to similar objects that have been encoded as implicit memories—stimulus-response without an agent to intervene.

Acting Agentically: Agency requires that one has acquired the capacity to know *implicitly* the intention behind the action or inaction, i.e. to know implicitly what the action is intended to accomplish.[11] Such intentions would have been learned either implicitly without awareness of it or learned explicitly and become implicit. And as we've seen, it also requires that one can regulate the affect driving the action. Let's look at an agentic act more closely.

It begins with the affective response to the object. If the affect is regulated, it completes its primary processing and is available for secondary-reflective processing. There must also be an awareness of what we intend to have happen so we can decide whether or not to act. Finally, one must have the reflective capacity to guide the action toward that goal. If the affect is dysregulated, it becomes dissociated and is thus unavailable for higher order processing.[12] The intention can't be formulated. Moreover, as we've seen, when dysregulated, we are without reflective processes and unable to intervene between affect and the action it urges[13] (See Figure 2.1).

The Development of Agency: Mentalization theory traces the development of a conscious mind capable of agency to the attachment relationship.

Fonagy et al. (2002) argue that the origins of agency are preverbal; that infants acquire an implicit awareness that their actions effect the physical and social environment, a primitive sense of oneself as an agent. More precisely, supported by mother-infant research, intersubjectivists propose that this primitive sense of one's agency derives from the mother's contingent responding. Such moments provide the infant with the experience of influencing its caretaker and with a delighted sense of its own efficacy. With sufficient frequency, such moments result in positive expectations that serve as a foundation for agentic functioning and as an incentive for exercising it (Fonagy et al., 2003; Naham, 1994; Pollack & Slavin, 1998; Sander, 1987; Stern, 1985).

As we've seen, while the regulation of affect is fundamental for agentic functioning, assessing our intentions is also critical. With the development of verbal-reflective processes and the capacity to represent mental states, we learn explicitly that intentions are part of the picture. The capacity to assess intentions is learned during a period in the attachment relationship when the child is discovering its mind. It learns that there are feelings *and thoughts* behind actions and that intentions are represented verbally as beliefs, desires, wishes, etc. It comes to understand that intentions are the products of mind, that they can be complex, and that the outcome of an action is not necessarily intentional.[14] Once an intention has been formulated explicitly, with experience, it becomes known implicitly (Fonagy et al., 2002).[15] The child also learns that intentions are known only to the owner of the mind, and that any assessment of an intention is an interpretation. A fully developed capacity to mentalize one's own and other's intentions is a crucial development enabling humans to cooperate, a key component of the cognitive revolution brought about by the evolution of reflective processes.

Summary: Let me summarize and elaborate a bit by reviewing the process of acting agentically. It begins with the affective response to the object. The affect must first be regulated so that it can go through its primary processing and is available for secondary processing if necessary. At the same time, one's intention must be assessed to see if it is adaptive to the situation. If the situation is recognized and if an adaptive response has been encoded in implicit-procedural memory, the automated response is activated without further ado. To this point, the processing of affect and intention has been implicit. But what if the situation is novel? Now, we can't be spontaneous, but must act deliberately. Left brain, verbal-reflective processes are brought to bear. The affect and intention are assessed explicitly, and we use this information to guide our action toward the intended outcome.

Let's now look at self-generation. Here again, primary and secondary systems are involved.

Self-Generation—Primary and Reflective Systems

In what follows self-generation refers to the capacity for dyadic and autonomous development of the self toward greater complexity and coherence. Like agency, it is an expected but undertheorized outcome of development and psychotherapy. Especially when treating patients with developmental arrests, we hope for them to internalize growth-generating aspects of the treatment. In this section, I describe primary and reflective systems devoted to self-generation. I begin with the primary system illuminated by Tronick (Tronick, 2004; Tronick et al., 1998). He describes a dyadic system that operates at the implicit level. It originates in infancy and continues throughout the lifespan. I will then argue that processing one's stream of consciousness is a reflective self-generating system. Like affect regulation and the capacities for intersubjectivity and agency, the capacities for dyadic and autonomous self-generation are developed in the attachment relationship.

The Primary Self-Generative System: Tronick proposes a dyadic self-generating system that operates at the primary, implicit level of mental life. He begins with the idea that complex, open, biological systems like us have an inborn mechanism of growth to offset their inherent tendency to deteriorate (entropy).[16] It fulfills a first principle of complex systems—to continuously increase in complexity and coherence. He goes on to argue that affect attunement, the intersubjective, simultaneous experiencing of an affect, induces growth generating states of "shared consciousness." Such moments are marked by a mutually experienced affective resonance (Schore, 1994), a felt sense of cognitive expansion (Tronick, 2004), and an awareness that the other is also experiencing it. Tronick argues that by sharing one another's states of consciousness, both parties acquire information about the thoughts and feelings of the other. For example, the mother, by synchronizing her affect state with the infant's and thus entering an analogous state of consciousness, acquires information about the infant's state, knows it implicitly and uses it to guide her in her regulatory interactions with it. At the same time, the infant is learning implicitly about the mother's more mature state, which includes information about and expands its understanding of itself.

The system is mediated by implicit communications and engenders implicit knowing. Two implicit-selves come together by synchronizing their affect states and thereby know implicitly one another's subjective experience. At the same time, they are increasing in complexity and coherence. Tronick puts it this way.

> At the moment when the dyadic system is created both partners experience an expansion of their own state of consciousness (brain organization). Their states of consciousness become dyadic and expand to incorporate elements of consciousness of the other in a new and more coherent form. At this moment of forming a dyadic state of consciousness, and for the duration of its existence, there must be something akin to a powerful experience of fulfillment as one paradoxically becomes larger than oneself.
>
> (1998, p. 296)

This implicit dyadic system continues to operate throughout the lifespan and has important implications for therapeutic action (Stern et al., 1998).

The experience generated by affect attunement and cognitive expansion is vitalizing—a positively toned, moderately hyper-aroused state. Schore (2011) argues that this pleasurable state is another aspect of attunement's contribution to therapeutic action, and that it offsets the negative aspects and encourages both the patient and the therapist to explore stressful topics. This on top of the other therapeutic effects of attunement that we saw above: the patient's experience of being recognized, the disposition toward empathy it generates in the therapist, the trust it engenders in the patient, and now we add that the positive hyper-arousal attunement generates supports the exploration of stressful topics. I think it's fair to say that affect attunement is the magic elixir of psychotherapy, in this case by generating growth-enhancing states of consciousness.

Let's now look at reflective, autonomous self-generation. In the absence of established ideas, I will speculate about the nature of the system, its original development, and its development in psychotherapy.

The Reflective Self-Generative System: Surprisingly, in the psychoanalytic literature only, Modell (1993) has addressed self-generation using reflective processes. However, he's interested in the capacity to sustain oneself in solitary states.[17] It's a kind of auto-regulation that is adjacent to, but different than the kind of self-generation to which Tronick referred and is my concern here—the ongoing process of increasing our complexity and coherence. In what follows, I argue that the processing of one's stream of consciousness serves as a reflective, self-generating system complementing the implicit, dyadic system described by Tronick. I will then propose that the reflective system develops as we acquire the capacity to convert our implicit thoughts into verbal expressions in a growth-supporting relationship, and that the internalization of such self-generative processes is a desired outcome of psychotherapy.

Here again I am indebted to the work of Russell Meares (2005, 2012a, 2012b, 2016). He builds on the work of William James. James (2001) was interested in, indeed defined the self as, a state of consciousness devoted to processing one's stream of consciousness. He called this unique reflective state of consciousness the "duplex self," a term I shall adopt. This "stream of subjective life," as James also referred to it, is the output of the primary self. We'll see that the duplex self involves a complex coordination of implicit and explicit processes by which the reflective-self assesses and responds to the output of the primary self.

Meares's career has been devoted to understanding the original development and, in its absence, the therapeutic development of the duplex self. He argues that its failure to develop is the central defect in borderline personalities and that without the capacity to process their stream of consciousness they are without a core around which experience is organized. They have no core self providing a sense of constancy.[18] Let's look more closely at the duplex self, at the processing of one's stream of consciousness.

The Duplex Self: By "processing our stream of consciousness," I am referring to the everyday experience of becoming absorbed in thinking about personal concerns. It often occurs when we're doing something automatically such as driving or walking, but it can happen anytime we don't need to devote our attention to something else. It's a default mode, sometimes called a resting state, subserved by a neural system called the "default mode network" (Meares, 2012). Importantly, it can also be done deliberately by turning out attention inward and allowing it to occur. Although they may also involve processing one's stream of consciousness, I'm not referring to fantasizing, such as a patient who as an adolescent would run home from school, close the door to her bedroom, and imagine marrying Paul McCartney, nor am I speaking of artistic endeavors. Rather, I'm referring to ordinary moments when we find ourselves engaged in processing a topic of personal concern that has come to mind spontaneously—that has been presented to us.

Unless impeded the stream of consciousness is always flowing.[19] It flows out of the subcortical structures of the right brain, out of the implicit unconscious (see Figure 2.3). Normally, it streams preconsciously in the background, available for reflective processing as needed. We regularly make quick reference to it in order to access our responses to objects. Here, however, I am referring to forays into the inner world of varying lengths, in which we find ourselves reflecting on the flow of thoughts and feelings about personal matters that come to us unbidden. As we observe and react to our stream of consciousness, each thought and feeling is followed by thoughts and feelings about or associated to them, which are followed by thoughts and feelings about or associated to them, and so on. It's a free-flowing conversation with oneself that goes on for as long as it lasts.[20]

Let me take a moment to distinguish processing one's stream of consciousness from free association in psychoanalysis. We'll see below that they share a growth-promoting dynamic, but for now let's look at two important differences. The contrast between them highlights important aspects of the duplex self. While free association begins with accessing one's stream of consciousness, the patient is tasked with conveying its contents explicitly to the therapist. When I'm processing my stream of consciousness, I'm left to my private musings. Moreover, if mine is typical, the raw material would often be difficult to decipher by anyone other than the stream's owner. Making it comprehensible to another person is constraining. Another difference is that free associating patients are told to disregard reality. However, again if I'm typical, left to ourselves we are very much concerned with reality. After all, these are personal concerns that are coming to mind.

Other than to emphasize how personal it is, James didn't write about the content, nor about any functions the duplex self might serve. As he advised and did himself, I will address these issues using my own stream of consciousness as "data," just as you will have no choice but to examine your own stream to verify my observations. This is not as easy as it might sound. We have only two levels of consciousness and the duplex self uses both. As you will discover, any attempt to observe the process of reflecting on one's stream of consciousness deactivates it. We can only know the experience in retrospect.

Let's begin with James's description of the processes involved. We'll see that he understood the dynamics of the stream as the presentation of a gestalt by the right brain, followed by an unpacking and exploration of it by the explicit processes of the left brain, which may be followed by the presentation of a new gestalt followed again by an unpacking and exploration of it by the explicit processes of the left, and so on. I should also mention that, at least in my case, it does not seem so neatly ordered as this description would suggest.

The Implicit and Explicit Processes of the Duplex Self: James (2001) compared the dynamics of the stream of consciousness with that of a bird's life, alternating between "flights" and then "perches" on branches of trees. Just as we've highlighted the speed of implicit processes versus the slowness of explicit processes, he focused on the "pace" by which thoughts form. Flights are fast, which we can understand to refer to gestalts that arrive in one fell swoop. Perches are drawn out processes such as occur when we explore gestalts using explicit thinking. He understood the gestalts to be "transitive," taking us suddenly from one topic to another, instantaneous flights from a perch on one branch to a perch on another. He understood the perches to be "substantive," the exploration of the topic presented in the gestalt, said differently, the submission of implicit knowing to explicit examination. So, James describes consciousness as a flow of mentation alternating between topics presented to us in the form of gestalts and their exploration by explicit processes. He describes how explicit processing will conclude suddenly, replaced by the next gestalt, which will then be explored until it is replaced by a fresh gestalt, and so on — flights and perches, flights and perches.[21]

Along with implicit and explicit processes operating in tandem, James noticed something else about the form of thinking in which the duplex self engages. He addressed the paradoxical quality of reflecting on one's stream of consciousness, paradoxical in the same say we saw in episodic memories—one experiences oneself simultaneously as both subject and object (Model, 1993). Let me explain.

James observed that as our thoughts emerge, they don't surprise us. They come as just as we expect them to "…thoughts connect as we feel them to be connected." (p. 155) We recognize them as our own. As with episodic memories in which "I" (subject) observes "me" (object) in the past, the experience of reflecting on the stream is "I," the observer, am reflecting on a flow of thoughts and feelings that I recognize as mine, indeed as me.

"I" am reflecting on "me." We'll see below that experiencing oneself as both subject and object is in and of itself growth promoting.

James does not address it, but we can add to his description that the duplex self is a spontaneous system. We enter into the duplex state spontaneously, the topics are presented to us spontaneously, the thoughts and feelings about them are spontaneous, and even the characters with who I speak are cast spontaneously. Recall that I've conceived of Schore's implicit self, as the primary level of Winnicott's true-spontaneous self. The duplex self is the reflective level of the true self. It is reflecting on the output of the implicit self as its reacts automatically to objects. It is reflecting on those reactions as they ascend from the unconscious to the conscious level, and it is responding to them spontaneously.[22] Note the correspondence of the state one is in when the duplex self is activated and Winnicott's notion of the state of "going on being": in which the infant is discovering itself by becoming aware of its spontaneous gestures.

James doesn't discuss what goes on in his perches, but, in my case, the exploration of the topic at hand is conducted by means of imaginary discussions with myself or with people I know or have known. These discussions require explicit-verbal-syntactical processes. When I'm speaking with myself, I have the experience that I am speaking with a "presence" that I know is me. When I'm speaking with others, I don't decide that it would be a good idea to consult with so-and-so. On the contrary, the person with whom I speak seems to be determined by whether the response to the previous thought is collaborative or critical, encouraging or inhibiting. It's as though I have an inner casting director. When I'm speaking with myself, I find myself sometimes playing a critical and sometimes a supportive role.

The Content of the Duplex Self: We've been focused on the processes of the duplex self. What can be said about the content of the stream of consciousness? James mentions only that it is subjective. I take this to mean not only that it's our personal take on things, but that it involves personal matters. It's certainly true in my case. When I have been drawn into my inner world and find myself processing my stream of consciousness, I have inevitably been presented with an issue of personal concern. Although they have varying degrees of urgency, all are concerns I deem in need of my attention. I'm always intensely interested in them. Issues of all types well up: desires, needs, conflicts, losses, anticipated problems, the well-being of loved ones, figuring out how to fit in an errand on the way home, thoughts about something I'm writing, and unfinished personal business of all kinds. Each arrives in the form of a gestalt that presents the issue which I then explore using explicit processes. Even the errand follows this pattern.

Let me emphasize that in presenting me with my personal concerns the right brain, which is serving up these topics, is doing what it does—directing my attention to salient objects, in this case personal issues in need of my attention. Also note that the gestalts served up by the right brain set the agenda for the explicit processes of the left brain that I use to explore whatever the issue may be. McGilchrist's seminal text, *The Emperor and His Emissary (2009)*, refers to this dynamic in its title. The right brain is the emperor setting the agenda for what the left brain does.

Among the issues presented, conflicts are of particular importance for self-generation.[23] They are impediments to growth, and their resolution often sets off growth spurts. In my case, conflicts seem to gnaw at me, and I gnaw at them until I'm presented with a solution or not.[24] Working through a conflict over time is also the work of the duplex self, and this also happens spontaneously. The same is true for working through loss. But growth requires more than the removal of obstacles. There are growth-supporting mechanisms that are part and parcel of the processing of our stream of consciousness.

Growth-Supporting Mechanisms Inherent to the Duplex Self: One of the self-generating mechanisms inherent to the duplex self is the coordination of implicit and explicit processing. It goes like this. First, I am presented with a personally salient issue. It is presented as a gestalt. The explicit processing that follows unpacks, breaks down, makes more differentiated, and thus increases the complexity of my understanding. This is then transferred back to the right brain where it is synthesized with what I already understand about the issue, thereby increasing the complexity of the gestalt that will be presented the next time the issue comes up. At the same time, the logic imposed by explicit processing supports the coherence of my understanding of the issue. We see in this an intrinsically growth-supporting mechanism. The coordinated operations of the right and left brains increase our complexity and coherence.

Another self-generating mechanism inherent to the duplex self is less obvious. In an important paper on therapeutic action, John Rosegrant (2005) illuminates a growth-promoting dynamic intrinsic to the process of free associating. The same dynamic is operative during the processing of one's stream of consciousness. Rosegrant understands free association to be an altered state of consciousness that is inherently growth promoting because it engenders an oscillation between "subject awareness" and "object awareness" (Bach, 1985). He argues that engaging in free association "...facilitates the patient's learning to integrate and to shift flexibly..." between these two perspectives. How so?

Recall that subject awareness refers to an awareness of one's own and other's subjective experience. It's a right brain-dominant state. Object awareness is a state of consciousness filled with experiencing oneself and others as objects—left brain dominant. These are key features of implicit versus explicit consciousness. Optimally the flexible shifting between them creates a balance. Rosegrant argues that when patients enter free associative states of consciousness, they have been primed by instructions such as to disregard reality, i.e. to enter highly subjective states of consciousness. However, they are always implicitly aware of the analyst's presence and the analyst represents an objective perspective. There is thus a tension between these polarities, and patients "... are always to some extent both subjectively and objectively self-aware, and ... always oscillating among degrees of relatively subjective self-awareness and degrees of relatively objective self-awareness" (p. 742). One's subjective, right brain-generated experience is always being tested against and integrated with an objective, left brain view, arguably resulting in increased complexity and coherence.

We can also see this subjective-objective dynamic in the process of speaking spontaneously with ourselves or imagined others. Like the analyst of the free-associating patient, the entity spoken with, ourself or others, represents the objective view. Moreover, speaking to these virtual entities entails sentences employing explicit, objectifying processes. Such fluctuations between implicit and explicit processing, and between subjective and objective states of consciousness provide the capacity not only for self-reflexivity (awareness of self and others as subjects and objects) (Aron, 2000) but also for increasing our complexity and coherence—for self-generation.

We'll see below that there is a third growth-promoting aspect of processing one's stream of consciousness—the attitude toward and the competence of the exploration. We'll see that these are learned—internalizations of attitude and competence of the attachment figures who guided the original explorations. Just as it's not a given that we are capable of reflecting on our stream of consciousness (Meares, 2005, 2012a), it is not a given that we will do so competently or with an attitude that supports development.

Let's now look at how the capacity to process one's stream of consciousness develops. It has important implications for how to develop the capacity in psychotherapy. This is what Russell Meares has illuminated. It starts to develop in the third year during a period in which the child begins to engage in what Piaget (1959) called "symbolic play."

The Development of the Duplex Self: Meares (2005) argues that the development of the capacity to process one's stream of consciousness begins with the mother participating in a particular type of play in which the child is imagining and expressing its thoughts as they come to mind. The mother attunes to the infant and joins its world. As Tronick has shown, attunement is the mother's gateway into the child's world and enables her to share the child's state of consciousness. She enters the infant's world unobtrusively and the child accepts her as part of it. It looks like this.

At first, as yet unable to form mental representations, the infant uses physical objects to represent its thoughts. Tall objects are mommies, smaller objects are the baby, cups may be rabbit holes. The mother fits herself into and participates in the child's reality. This is what Meares calls the "play space." It is a transitional space (Winnicott, 1953) where the infant and mother share a reality presented by the infant. Note that the method of representation is analogical. Tall objects are like the mommy. Cups are like rabbit holes. The right brain, comparing patterns, is dominant. The sentence producing left brain has only just begun to develop. Meares emphasizes that, along with her affect attunement, by accepting the analogies, the mother is engaging in "representational attunement."

Piaget illustrates such play at a slightly later point with a child representing its thoughts by drawing with its mother by its side. Now we see something more going on. We see that the child is talking to itself out loud in the presence of an attuned other. It is speaking its thoughts as they stream into consciousness.

There, I'm drawing in this sheet. I'm making a funny man. What am I doing? It's a waterworks. Here I must draw the water. Now the water. I'll make a boat too. A little boat and an Indian, a man and a woman, two men and a woman. Two men and an Indian. They've fallen into the water you see.

(Piaget, 1959, p. 242)

Piaget notes that the child is not attempting to engage in dialogue, but rather is engaging in soliloquy spoken to himself. The "you" he mentions at the end is him. However, Piaget goes on.

> What he says does not seem *to him* to be addressed to himself but is enveloped with the feeling of a *presence*, so that to speak of himself or to speak to his mother appear to be the same thing. .... one cannot but be struck by the soliloquist character of these same remarks. The child does not ask questions and expects no answer, neither does he attempt to give any definite information to his mother who is present. He does not ask himself whether she is listening or not. *He speaks for himself just as an adult does when he speaks within himself.*
>
> (Piaget, 1959, p. 243, my italics)

This shared consciousness of the play space is the precursor of the duplex self. The soliloquy of the child is his expression of his thoughts as they emerge, his stream of consciousness. The mother's presence and enabling functions are internalized. The enabling functions include her affective and representational attunement.[25] Like Winnicott's mother interacting around a transitional object, she speaks from within the child's reality and doesn't interrupt it. Rather, she fits herself in, and the child accepts her as part of his consciousness. She becomes a background presence reflecting on what the child says as he speaks what comes into consciousness. She will be internalized as the "I" reflecting on "my thoughts," on "me."

We see the same approach by the mother as the child's cognitive capacities develop and as it becomes more social and concerned with its own and other's mental states, as it begins to learn to mentalize. What began in play becomes deadly serious as the child seeks help in processing its socioemotional concerns, everything from the slights of siblings, to not getting its own way, to being empathic with others. Now the mother is tasked with both affective and representational attunement, with helping the child stay regulated while joining the child in its private socioemotional world to help in the representation of mental states. And there is something more, most of which is conveyed and learned implicitly. Consider this.

At the same time that the child is acquiring the capacity to represent its own and other's mental states, it is also developing an attitude toward and competence in exploring them. Ideally, the attitude includes curiosity, intrepidness, and positive expectations. The competence depends on an understanding of how the mind works conveyed by the mother and on her role as a "guide." First and foremost, she listens receptively and empathically, but occasionally she will point toward and formulate salient issues not appreciated by the child. She will provide ways of understanding them that convey an understanding of how the mind works, and she will ask questions that encourage the child to discover its own thoughts about the matter at hand.

I'm speculating of course, but perhaps not wildly. I think of the mother as guide, because of a way of working that emerged as I became influenced by regulation theory and by Meares's understanding of the development of the duplex self.[26] I found myself acting in the role of guide like the one I assigned to the mother, pointing to unnoticed relevant issues, providing language for representing mental states, conveying an understanding of how the mind operates, and, always, encouraging exploration by discovery of one's own thoughts about the matter at hand. I can assume the role of guide once the patient has begun to speak their mind spontaneously, as the thoughts come to it. This begins once my intentions and emotional competency are trusted and after regulatory processes have improved sufficiently for a patient to tolerate the affect associated with the content of the stream.

Once spontaneous speaking starts, I find myself speaking less and less. I listen in as an attuned a way as possible. The attunement generates a flow and a shared absorption that I hesitate to interrupt. Note that speaking less is not to say that I communicate less. The communication is nonverbal. I convey intense interest. My matched affect states convey recognition. The felt resonances and sense of closeness coming from my attunement mark that I have sampled and am aware of the patients' experience — that I recognize and have entered their subjective world. We are in Meares's play space. Like the soliloquizing child Piaget describes, patients are often talking to me and to themselves simultaneously. There are moments when this is intense enough so that I suspect that like the mother I fade into the background. One patient who had begun to speak spontaneously told me, laughing at herself, that she realized she was using therapy to find out what she really thinks.

I believe that my ongoing affect attunement encourages spontaneous speech. The nurturing disposition that attunement creates in me is conveyed implicitly to the patient. The attunement simultaneously generates a sense of being recognized. Together, my nurturing disposition and the patient's sense of being recognized engender trust. Recall also that affect attunement generates states of positive, moderate hyper-arousal that offset negative states and fuels further exploration. Perhaps most importantly, there is an intimacy and warmth, dare I say love, that infuses the bond. And I've also noticed this. Because I am attuned to the patient's subjective experience and feel nurturant, I can trust my responses to be growth promoting and I too allow myself to speak spontaneously.

Speaking spontaneously in therapy requires that the patient trusts the emotional competence of the therapist, not only in the sense of attuning and keeping them in regulated states, but also to help them competently navigate the intrapsychic and intersubjective terrains, to act as a guide, sometimes pointing out fruitful issues, sometimes reflecting their experience back to them, sometimes commenting nonverbally, sometimes verbally, but always encouraging them to explore further. My questions and directions aim to turn their attention to their stream of consciousness, to the spontaneous thoughts that emerge. I often say things like "Say more." to encourage them to further explore and issue. If I ask a question to which they respond, "I don't know." I might say, "Well, what are your thoughts about it." I ask things like "What's your take on it?" I sometimes ask, "What do you want to have happen?" focusing them on their intentions.

I see my role as directing patients' attention toward their spontaneous thoughts as they arrive and guiding them in exploring where they go. I believe that these kinds of interactions help to develop the inclination and capacity to process their stream of consciousness. The therapeutic stance I've described here overlaps with those described by Grossmark (2018) who "accompanies" his patients "unobtrusively," by Ringstrom (2001) who engages his patients in "improvisational" interactions that encourage spontaneity, and by Kaufmann (2023) who notes how empathy opens his patients.

Let me end with this. Harold Bloom (1998) argues the Shakespeare invented the human. I'm not qualified to comment on this, but I want to draw your attention to what he says about Shakespeare's understanding of what is distinctive about being a human. In the opening sentence of the book, Bloom asserts:

> Literary character before Shakespeare is relatively unchanging; women and men are represented as aging and dying, but not as changing because their relationship to themselves, rather than to the gods or God, has changed. In Shakespeare characters develop rather than unfold, and they develop because they reconceive themselves. Sometimes this comes about because they *overhear* themselves talking, whether to themselves

or to others. Self-overhearing is their royal road to individuation, and no other writer, before or since Shakespeare, has accomplished so well the virtual miracle of creating utterly different yet self-consistent voices for his more than one hundred major characters and many hundreds of highly distinctive minor personages.

(Original italics. p. XIX)

Put in our terms, Shakespeare invented an array of unique characters, each with an inner world in which they spoke with themselves and others. Overhearing these conversations fostered self-generation.

Summary and Conclusion: I have proposed a model of the core self as the locus and maker of subjective experience, and as the performer of functions. I've argued that affect establishes our subjective experience of objects, what they mean to us, by grounding meaning experientially in the body. I've proposed four functions of central clinical interest: the regulation of affect, intersubjective relating, agentic functioning, and self-generation. The self performs these functions using primary-implicit and reflective-secondary-explicit processes.

Affect Regulation: The regulation of affect is foundational. All other functions depend on it. There is a primary-neurobiological system that operates unconsciously and regulates affect automatically and a verbal-reflective, mentalization system that operates consciously and regulates affect deliberately. *Intersubjectivity:* Primary intersubjectivity is accomplished through the real-time implicit detection and responding to one's own and other's affect states. Secondary intersubjectivity is accomplished using verbal-reflective processes to assess one's own and other's mental states that have occurred or are anticipated. *Agency:* Acting agentically is understood as the capacity to direct one's actions toward intended goals in real time. It requires that affect is regulated, that it can be assessed to know one's intentions, and that its regulation allows mastery over one's actions. It uses a mixture of implicit and explicit processes. *Self-generation:* At the implicit level, self-generation requires the capacity to engage in shared states of consciousness. At the reflective level, it involves the autonomous processing of one's stream of consciousness. Finally, I have proposed a therapeutic technique aimed at fostering the capacity and propensity to process one's stream of consciousness.

Of course, all of this and more goes awry when affect is dysregulated. Just as self-functioning is impaired by dysregulation, consciousness and self-experience become disordered, the topics of Chapter 4.

Notes

1 Bromberg writes, "Self-states are highly individualized modules of being, each configured by its own organization of cognition, beliefs, dominant affect and mood, access to memory, skills, behaviors, values, actions and regulatory physiology" (2008, p. 73).
2 This is actually to say that the mind, of which the self is a feature, originates in the body. The idea goes back at least as far as Freud who said that the ego was first and foremost a body **ego** (1923), and James who understood the psychological self to originate in the "material self" (2004).
3 Meares has conducted research in New Zealand on the effectiveness of a technique he calls the Conversational Model (2012b). Although it has not been studied as extensively, results are comparable to those of Mentalization-Based Treatment and Dialectical Behavioral Therapy for the treatment of borderline personality disorder.
4 Intersubjective theory had far-reaching implications. For example, clinical phenomena were now understood to be the creation of two individual subjectivities— a "third thing" that is an emergent product of the intersubjective field and unique to that relationship. Enactments became central to clinical work (Benjamin, 2004; Bromberg, 1998, 2006; Ogden, 1994, 2004).
5 Intersubjective theory found empirical confirmation in research that examined split second mother-infant interactions and supported the idea that the capacity for intersubjectivity originates in the mother-infant relationship and is central to the formation of the early attachment relationship. Stern (1977, 1986) showed the criticality of affect attunement in the development of intersubjective engagement. Feldman (1999, 2007, 2011) illuminated the importance of synchronization in the intersubjective process. Trevarthan showed the progression from what he called primary to secondary intersubjectivity (1977, 1993; Trevarthen & Aitken, 2001). Lyons-Ruth (1999) and Beebe and Lachman (1998, 1994) explored the roles of action sequences or what Lyons-Ruth called "relational moves." Beebe and her colleagues (2012) found that relational patterns established by four months were able to predict disorganized attachment. Shore's integration of mother-infant research (1994) with attachment theory and neurobiology gave further support to the proposal that the primary intersubjective system mediates early attachment experiences resulting in secure versus insecure outcomes.
6 Arguably, the infant arrives primed for this with an innate, unfolding capacity to respond to the sights and sounds that make up the implicit communications by which we convey our affect states (Stern, 1977; Trevarthan, 1993).

7 They become our spontaneous, real-time, split-second ways of interacting that comprise our "working model of attachment," and predict secure and insecure attachment.

8 This has been given further support with the advance of "hyper-scanning," the measuring of neural activity in patient and therapist simultaneously, and in which right brain activity becomes synchronized. This synchronization is performed by the right lateralized temporoparietal junction (Schore, 2019a, 2021). See also Koole and Tschacher (2016) who look at the role of synchrony in the therapeutic alliance.

9 Likewise the therapeutic action for modifying the implicit systems is new experiences in a relationship, whereas the mentalizing system is developed through talking about mental states.

10 One way of thinking about the difference is that one's definition of agency depends on whether the problem is understood with regard to the implicit or the repressed unconscious (Craparo & Mucci, 2017).

11 Here again we see the primacy of affect, not only in the fact that that mastery of our actions relies on regulated affect, but also in the fact that all intentions originate in affect (Fonagy et al., 2002; Jurist, 2005).

12 We also develop dissociation, which began as a symptom of dysregulation, as a defense against it. Subsequently, it is activated in anticipation of becoming dysregulated.

13 In any case, when dysregulated, we lose reflective capacities, so even if the affect were processed at the primary level, we wouldn't be able to do the secondary processing.

14 It learns, for example, that saying something that is wrong is not necessarily lying, and that one can step on someone's foot accidently.

15 Others, me included, would question this. Based on the idea of implicit learning and the idea of implicit knowing developed by the Boston Change Process Study Group, I think it's likely that the infants learn about intentions implicitly and explicitly. For our purposes this doesn't matter. The point is that the capacity to represent intentions must be developed.

16 In biology, the inherent capacity of living things to maintain and renew themselves at the cellular level is called autopoiesis.

17 Drawing from examples of those who survived solitary confinement without trauma and artists working alone, he finds that such self-sustenance is enabled by personal passions and intense moral commitments, often with the help of vitalizing internal objects such as mothers or muses or a mix of the two.

18 His research has demonstrated the effectiveness of what he calls the Conversational Method as a treatment developing the duplex self in borderline personalities. It's far more complex and nuanced than its name implies.

19 Meares notes that it provides ongoing sense of our personal existence, an "authentic feeling of being alive" (Meares, 2005, 2012a).

20 Meares (2012) argues that this system is subserved by the default mode net-work, a heavily researched neural system that is activated when there are no demands on our attention, when we are not involved in a task requiring delib-erate thinking, and when we're in an introspective state (Raichle et al., 2001). Interestingly, it also consumes a disproportionate amount of neural energy. Meares documents that it is associated with activities associated with the self, activities such as the activation of autobiographical memory and exercising "theory of mind." Importantly for what follows, it is also associated with spon-taneous cognition (Andrew-Hannah et al., 2010).

21 In my case, the new gestalt sometimes furthers the exploration of the origi-nal topic with a new thought about it, and sometimes presents an associated topic—associated because it is like it. The associated topic often has the same pattern. It is analogous. An example would be that I'm exploring what hap-pened in a relationship and I switch to thinking about another relationship that has the same pattern.

22 Recall that Schore's implicit self, the limbic-autonomic system, mediates our initial, automatic responses to objects based on past experience with them. It is the "implicit unconscious" out of which flows the stream of consciousness.

23 I am referring to both moral conflicts and those stemming from ambivalence about self and objects.

24 From what I can tell, the solutions are usually arrived at unconsciously and come to me all at once as insights, although, given that no conflict seems too trivial to get my attention, that word may be a bit lofty much of the time.

25 Representational attunement is at the heart of Meares's Conversational Model. In a nutshell, it involves responding analogically. The mother's analogical responding is in keeping with the child's stage of development. The child's left brain has only just begun to develop. The right brain is dominant, and thus, the child thinks in analogies. The Conversational Model applies this approach to patients with borderline personality disorders.

26 Recall that Meares's Conversational Model is devoted to borderline patients who haven't developed the capacity to process their stream of consciousness at all. I am describing a techique suitable for higher functioning patients, those with structured insecure attachment patterns rather than the disorganized pat-terns typical of borderline personalities.

Bibliography

Allen, J., & Fonagy, P. (Eds.). (2006). *Handbook of mentalization-based treatment*. Chichister: John Wiley Sons Ltd.

Allen, J., Fonagy, P., & Batemen, A. (2008). *Mentalizing in clinical practice*. Arlington, VA: American Psychiatric Publishing, Inc.

Andrews-Hanna, J. R., Reidler, J. S., Huang, C., Randy, L., & Buckner, R. L. (2010). Evidence for the default network's role in spontaneous cognition. *Journal of Neurophysiology, 104*, 322–335.

Aron, L. (1991). The patient's experience of the analyst's subjectivity. *Psychoanalytic Dialogues, 1*, 29–51.

Aron, L (2000). Self-reflexivity and the therapeutic action of psychoanalysis. *Psychoanalytic Psychology, 17*(4), 667–689.

Bach, S. (1985). *Narcissistic states and the therapeutic process.* New York: Jason Aronson.

Bandura, A. (2018). Toward a psychology of human agency: Pathways and reflections. *Perspectives on Psychological Science, 13*(2), 130–136.

Bass, A. (2019). Memories and reflections on my life in relational psychoanalysis. *Psychoanalytic Inquiry, 39*, 114–122.

Beebe, B., & Lachmann, F. M. (1988). The contribution of mother-infant mutual influence to the origins of self- and object representations. *Psychoanalytic Psychology, 5*(4), 305–337.

Beebe, B., & Lachmann, F. M. (1994). Representation and internalization in infancy: Three principles of salience. *Psychoanalytic Psychology, 11*, 127–165.

Beebe, B., & Lachman, F. (2002). *The origins of attachment: Infant research and adult treatment.* New York: Routledge.

Beebe, B., Lachmann, F., Markese, S., & Bahrick, L. (2012). On the origins of disorganized attachment and internal working models: Paper I. A dyadic systems approach. *Psychoanalytic Dialogues, 22*, 253–272.

Benjamin, J. (1988). *The bonds of love.* New York: Pantheon Books.

Benjamin, J. (1990). An outline of intersubjectivity: The development of recognition. *Psychoanalytic Psychology, 7*, 33–46.

Benjamin J (2004). Beyond doer and done to: An intersubjective view of thirdness. *Psychoanalytic Quarterly, 73*, 5–46.

Bettleheim, B. (1982). *Freud and man's soul.* New York: Random House.

Bloom, H. (1998). *Shakespeare: The invention of the human.* New York: Riverhead Books.

Bromberg, P. (1998). *Standing in the spaces.* Hillsdale, NJ: The Analytic Press, Inc.

Bromberg, P. (2006). *Awakening the dreamer: Clinical journeys.* Mahwah, NJ: Analytic Press.

Bromberg, P. M. (2008). Shrinking the Tsunami: Affect regulation, dissociation, and the shadow of the flood*. *Contemporary Psychoanalysis, 44*, 329–350.

Crapara, G., & Mucci, C. (2017). *Unrepressed unconscious, implicit memory, and clinical work.* London. Karnac Books.

Damasio, A. (2010). *Self comes to mind: Constructing the conscious brain.* New York: Pantheon.

Edelman, G. (2004). *Wider than the Sky; the phenomenal gift of consciousness.* New Haven, CT: Yale Books.

Feldman, R., Greenbaum, C. W., & Yirmiya, N. (1999). Mother-infant affect synchrony as an antecedent of the emergence of self-control. *Developmental Psychology, 35*, 223–231. doi:10.1037/0012-1649.35.1.223

Feldman, R. (2007). Parent-infant synchrony and the construction of shared timing; physiological precursors, developmental outcomes, and risk conditions. *Journal of Child Psychology and Psychiatry, 48*, 329–354.

Feldman, R., Magori-Cohen, R., Galili, G., Singer, M., & Louzon, Y. (2011). Mother and infant coordinate heart rhythms through episodes of interaction synchrony. *Infant Behavior and Development, 34*, 569–577. doi:10.1016/j.infbeh.2011.06.008

Fonagy, P., Gergely, G., Jurist, E., & Target, M. (2002). *Affect regulation, mentalization, and the development of the self.* New York: Other Press.

Fonagy, P., Target, M., Gergely, G., Allen, J. G., & Bateman, A. W. (2003). The developmental roots of borderline personality disorder in early attachment relationships: A theory and some evidence. *Psychoanalytic Inquiry, 23*(3), 412–459.

Freud, S. (1923). The ego and the Id. In *Standard edition of the complete psychological works of Sigmund Freud* (Vol. 19). London: Hogarth Press.

Grossmark, R. (2018). *The unobtrusive relational analyst: Explorations in psychoanalytic companioning.* New York: Routledge.

James, W. (2001). *Psychology: The briefer course.* New York: Dover Publications.

Jurist, E. (2005). Mentalized affectivity. *Psychoanalytic Psychology, 22*, 426–444.

Kaufmann, P. (2023) When empathy opens. *Psychoanalytic Perspectives, 20*, 331–350.

Koole, S. L., & Tschacher, W. (2016). Synchrony in psychotherapy: A review and an integrative framework for the therapeutic alliance. *Frontiers in Psychology, 7*, 862. doi:10.3389/fpsyg.2016.00862

Kuchuck, S. (2020). *The relational revolution in psychoanalysis and psychotherapy.* New York: Routledge.

Lyons-Ruth, K. (1999). The two-person unconscious: Intersubjective dialogue, enactive relational representation, and the emergence of new forms of relational organization. *Psychoanalytic Inquiry, 19*, 576–617. doi:10.1080/07351699909534267

Lyons-Ruth, K., Bruschweiler-Stern, N., Harrison, A. M., Nahum, J. P., Sander, L., Stern, D. N., & Tronick E. Z. (1998). Implicit relational knowing: Its role in development and psychoanalytic treatment. *Infant Mental Health Journal, 19*, 282–289.

Meares, R. (2005). *The metaphor of play: Origin and breakdown of personal being.* New York: Routledge.

Meares, R. (2012a). *A dissociation model of borderline personality disorder.* New York: Norton.

Meares, R. (2012b). *Borderline personality disorder and the conversational model: A clinician's manual.* New York: Norton.

Meares, R. (2016). *The poet's voice in the making of mind.* New York: Routledge.

Modell, A. (1993). *The private self.* New York: Harvard University Press.

McGilchrist, I. (2009). *The Master and his Emissary: The divided brain and the making of the western world.* New Haven, CT: Yale University Press.

Nahum, J. P. (1994). New theoretical vistas in psychoanalysis: Louis Sander's theory of early development. *Psychoanalytic Psychology, 11*, 1–19.

Ogden, T. H. (1994). The analytic third: Working with intersubjective clinical facts. *The International Journal of Psychoanalysis, 75*, 319.

Ogden, T. H. (2004). The analytic third: Implications for psychoanalytic theory and technique. *Psychoanalysis Quarterly, 73*, 167–195.

Piaget, J. (1959). *The language and thought of the child* (3rd edition). London: Routledge & Kegan Paul.

Pollock, L., & Slavin, J. H. (1998). The struggle for recognition: Disruption and reintegration in the experience of agency. *Psychoanalytic Dialogues, 8*, 857–873.

Raichle, M. E., MacLeod, A. M., Snyder, A. Z., Powers, W. J., Gusnard, D. A., & Shulman, G. L. (2001). Inaugural article: A default mode of brain function. *Proceedings of the National Academy of Sciences, 98*(2), 676–682.

Rakoczy, H. (2022). Foundations of theory of mind and its development in early childhood. *Nature Reviews Psychology, 1*, 223–235.

Ringstrom, P. (2001). Cultivating the improvisational in psychoanalytic treatment. *Psychoanalytic Dialogues, 11*(5), 727–754.

Rosegrant, J. (2005). The therapeutic effects of the free-associative state of consciousness. *Psychoanalytic Quarterly, 74*, 737–766.

Sander, L. (1987). A 25 year follow-up: Some reflections on personality development over the long term. *Infant Mental Health, 8*, 210–220.

Schore, A. N. (1994). *Affect regulation and the origin of the self: The neurobiology of emotional development.* New York: Norton.

Schore, A. N. (2003). *Affect regulation and the repair of the self.* New York: Norton.

Schore, A. N. (2009). Right brain affect regulation: An essential mechanism of development, trauma, dissociation and psychotherapy. In D. Fosha, M. Solomon & D. Siegel (Eds.), *The healing power of emotion: A dialogue among scientists and clinicians. Integrating relationships, body and mind* (pp. 112–144). New York: Norton.

Schore, A. N. (2010). The right brain implicit-self: A central mechanism of the psychotherapy change process. In J. Petrucelli (Ed.), *Knowing, not knowing and sort of knowing* (pp. 177–202). London: Karnac Books Ltd.

Schore, A. N. (2011). The right brain implicit-self lies at the core of psychoanalysis. *Psychoanalytic Dialogues, 21*, 1–26.

Schore, A. N. (2012). *The science of the art of psychotherapy.* New York: Norton.

Schore, A. N. (2017). The right brain implicit-self: A central mechanism of the psychotherapy change process. In G. Craparo & C. Mucci (Eds.), *Unrepressed unconscious, implicit memory and clinical work* (pp. 73–98). London: Karnac.

Schore, A. N. (2019a). *Right brain psychotherapy.* New York: Norton.

Schore, A. N. (2019b). *The development of the unconscious mind.* New York: Norton.

Schore, A. N. (2021). The interpersonal neurobiology of intersubjectivity. *Frontiers in Psychology, 12*, 648616. doi:10.3389/fpsyg.2021.648616

Stern, D. N. (1977). *The first relationship.* Cambridge, MA: Harvard University Press.

Stern, D. N. (1985). *The interpersonal world of the child.* New York: Basic Books.

Stern, D. N., Sander, L. W., Nahum, J. P., Harrison, A. M., Lyons-Ruth, K., Morgan, A. C., Bruschweiler-Stern, N., & Tronick, E. Z. (1998). Non-interpretive mechanisms in psychoanalytic therapy: The 'something more' than interpretation. *International Journal of Psychoanalysis, 79*, 903–921.

Stolorow, R., Brandchaft, B., & Atwood, G. (1987). *Psychoanalytic treatment: An intersubjective approach*. Hillsdale, NJ: The Analytic Press.

Trevarthen, C. (1979). Communication and cooperation in early infancy. A description of primary intersubjectivity. In M. M. Bullows (Ed.), *Before speech: The beginning of interpersonal communication* (pp. 321–348). New York: Cambridge University Press.

Trevarthen, C. (1993). The self born in intersubjectivity: The psychology of an infant communicating. In U. Neisser (Ed.), *The perceived self: Ecological and interpersonal sources of self-knowledge* (pp. 121–173). New York: Cambridge University Press.

Trevarthen, C., & Aitken, K. J. (2001). Infant intersubjectivity: Research, theory, and practice. *Journal of Child Psychology Psychiatry, 42*, 3–48.

Tronick, E., & the Boston Change Process Study Group. (1998). Dyadically expanded states of consciousness and the process of therapeutic change. *Infant Mental Health Journal, 19*(3), 290–299.

Tronick, E. (2004). Why is connection with others so critical? The formation of dyadic states of consciousness and the expansion of individuals' states of consciousness. In E. Tronick (Ed.), *The neurobehavioral and social-emotional development of infants and children* (pp. 476–499). New York: Norton.

Winnicott, D. W. (1953). Transitional objects and transitional phenomena: A study of the first not-me possession. *The International Journal of Psychoanalysis, 34*, 89–97.

Winnicott, D. W. (1960). Ego distortion in terms of true and false self. In *The maturational process and the facilitating environment: Studies in the theory of emotional development* (pp. 140–157). New York: International Universities Press, Inc.

Chapter 4

Being Dysregulated
Disordered Consciousness and Disordered Self

We have seen that dysregulation results in dissociated affect and how problematic that is for self-functioning. We've also seen that dysregulation impairs reflective processing, further contributing to our dysfunctionality. Without affective information and reflective processes, one is unable to assess one's own subjective experience, unable interact intersubjectively, unable to act agentically, and unable to engage in self-generation. Becoming dysregulated at low levels of stress results in chronically impaired functionality and in developmental arrests.

In this chapter, I focus on the experience of being dysregulated. We will see that when affect is dysregulated, consciousness becomes disordered, and as expected, we'll see that disordered consciousness comes with a disordered sense of self, the other side of the coin. I will focus on moderate dysregulation, typical of those with structured insecure attachment (preoccupied and avoidant). When dysregulated, they experience a moderately disordered state of consciousness and a moderately disordered sense of self. The type of disordering depends on whether the dysregulation is hyper- or hypo-aroused. Such disorders of consciousness are marked by *disturbances in the relationship to experience, a reduction of the complexity of consciousness*, and a *breakdown of coherence*. Along with disordered consciousness, dysregulation is marked by disturbances in the sense of self. Depending on the type of dysregulation, the self is experienced as fragmented or empty. Given the number of patients with structured insecure attachment, such states of moderately disordered consciousness have not received the attention they deserve.

Traumatology has focused on flashbacks and depersonalization-derealization, severely disordered states of consciousness that accompany severe states of dysregulation. There are, however, degrees of dysregulation

DOI: 10.4324/9781003266617-5

and a corresponding spectrum of the impairments to consciousness. Perhaps the neglect is due to the fact that severely disordered consciousness is disabling and obvious, whereas moderately disordered consciousness is "merely" debilitating, often undetected by others, and often so subtle that it is undetected by oneself except in retrospect.

Schore (1994, 2012) notes that disordered states of consciousness are important factors in developmental arrests and that they impede therapeutic progress. For those who become dysregulated at low levels of stress, moderately disordered consciousness is a frequent occurrence. When thinking about stressful material, moderately impaired states of consciousness impede patients' capacity to think and feel clearly and fully. Moreover, they are unable to reflect on and integrate whatever thoughts and feelings they may have. As mentioned in Chapter 3, the self-generative function is impaired by the incapacity to process stressful material.

There is consensus that discussion of disordered consciousness is critical when treating severe dissociative disorders (Ataria, 2014; Chefetz, 2015; Dell, 2009a). This is true for moderate dissociative disorders as well. For the therapist, appreciating the cognitive impact and subjective experience of dysregulation guides empathic responses. For patients, although they are inevitably aware of their chronically disordered states of consciousness, it is rarely brought up as a concern or thought about in a constructive way. Patients often find such states frightening and/or shameful. In many cases, I've learned of a patient's impaired state only because I was cued by my own matched or reactive state, or when they say something like "Is this making sense?" or "I know I'm all over the place." or when they report or when I surmise that their mind has gone blank. Yet, in my experience, when dysregulated-disordered states of consciousness are mentalized, it inevitably proves helpful. The experience of disordered consciousness often provides the first awareness that one is dysregulated. Also, recognizing disordered states of consciousness for what they are—symptoms of dysregulation— can serve to ameliorate shame about them, along with an understanding that the solution to the problem is the capacity to self-regulate.

Some background on the study of altered states of consciousness will help clarify key issues. The first general study of altered states of consciousness was *The Varieties of Religious Experience* by William James (1902).

He distinguished them from what he called "rational consciousness," today called "normal waking consciousness." Altered states involve a qualitatively different, temporary way of experiencing our inner and outer worlds. They may be drug induced, psychologically or behaviorally induced (meditation or physical exhaustion), intersubjectively induced (shared-expanded states of consciousness), physiologically induced (starvation, high fever), hypnotically induced, or trauma induced (peritraumatic altered states of consciousness), or, as with the ones we're discussing, they may be sequelae of trauma (Vaitl et al., 2005). That is, in the case of chronic moderately disordered states of consciousness, they are sequelae of early attachment trauma that has impaired the capacity to regulate affect and thus results in dysregulation at low levels of stress. Such impairment results in frequent moderate dysregulation and frequent moderately disordered consciousness.

Beginning with studies of "hypnoid states (Breuer & Freud, 1893/1955; Janet, 1889, 1901)" to the present (For an excellent overview see Dell, 2009b), it has been observed that altered states of consciousness are accompanied by "automatisms." Automaticity was originally observed in the conversion symptoms of "hysterics" who were subject to losing volitional control over their bodies and manifesting involuntary gestures or paralysis. ("Hysterics" are now understood to have been traumatized.) Janet noticed that when his patients were automatized, they were also in a "narrowed," or what today is thought of as a constricted state of consciousness. More recently, Bromberg (2006) noted that dissociated states accompany enactments comprised of involuntary interactions. In Chapter 2, I discussed constricted states in terms of the collapse of reflective processes that occurs when dysregulated. I also discussed automaticity as the breakdown of agency due to the deactivation of reflective processes and the activation of scripted responses that occurs when we are dysregulated. Let's now discuss the different types of disordered consciousness that occur depending on whether the dysregulated affect is hyper- or hypo-aroused.

The Different Effects of Hyper- and Hypo-aroused Dysregulation on Consciousness: Moderate Versus Severe

We've seen that early attachment trauma biases the limbic-autonomic nervous system toward either hyper- or hypo-arousal.[1] As a result, the response to stress is either hyper- *or* hypo-aroused rather than a capacity to respond flexibly depending on the situation. We've also seen that hyper- and hypo-arousal have starkly different effects on our states of consciousness. Hyper-arousal activates the right brain, which processes the present and generates implicit states of consciousness including a heightened subject awareness. Moderate arousal activates the left brain, which processes the past and future and generates explicit conscious-ness including a heightened object awareness. Our state of consciousness changes adaptively with our affective response to objects. That is, just as getting the affective response to the object right gets the relationship right, getting the affect right also generates the state of consciousness suitable for the task at hand. We've discussed this with regard to the different effects of regulated hyper- and hypo-arousal on normal waking consciousness.

We'll now see that dysregulated hyper- and hypo-arousal generate disor-dered states of consciousness that are phenomenologically opposites. Note, however, that both undergo a breakdown in the complexity and coherence of consciousness, and both suffer a degraded capacity for agentic thinking and acting. I will start with the phenomenological differences as seen in the severe disorders of consciousness and then compare them with moderately disordered states.

There are two types of PTSD. They were found to have distinct neural profiles.[2] One type is subject to triggered states of extreme hyper-aroused dysregulation. The other is subject to states of extreme hypo-aroused dysregulation. They manifest as dramatically different alterations of con-sciousness (Lanius et al., 2007, 2010, 2012; Stein et al., 2013; Wolf et al., 2012).[3] Patients with hyper-aroused PTSD experience flashbacks—*total immersion* in the experience of an activated memory. Those suffering the hypo-aroused type of PTSD experience depersonalization-derealization—*total detachment* from experience of the present.[4]

Moderately versus severely disordered states of consciousness: The degree of dysregulation is a key factor influencing the extent to which states of consciousness are altered (see, e.g., Dell, 2009a, 2009b; Frewen & Lanius, 2015). Whereas those with PTSD suffer severe dysregulation and severe impairments of consciousness, those suffering the sequelae of avoidant and preoccupied attachment trauma,[5] which might be called "ptsd," experience relatively moderate dysregulation and relatively moderate impairments of consciousness.[6] To compare moderate versus severe conditions, I'll continue to discuss involuntary immersion and detachment, keeping in mind that this is only one of the dimensions of disordered consciousness we'll be looking at. Let's start with involuntary immersion.

A full-on flashback sweeps one into in a memory to such an extent that it is experienced as the present—extreme hyper-arousal and thus extreme right brain. We see such immersion in a more moderate form, without the break with reality, when a memory is activated and sweeps us into it for a moment but is experienced as a memory—a partial immersion. Of course, it is not only memories in which we may become involuntarily immersed. We become involuntarily immersed in the present, without the capacity to pull back from it, when in states of dysregulated hyper-arousal. Impulsive actions occur in immersed states of consciousness.

Involuntary detachment is generated by dysregulated hypo-arousal and is mediated by the left brain. Depersonalization and derealization are states of extreme detachment, severely altered states of consciousness in which we experience ourselves outside of our body and/or states in which reality is experienced as distanced to the point of seeming unreal—full detachment. A partial, moderate form of involuntary detachment involves an objectification of and felt distance from self and others without the extreme sense of estrangement and alteration of perception. Such a moderately detached state of consciousness may not be experienced as particularly odd in and of themselves. Recall that we routinely go in and out of being in-the-moment and stepping back it. They don't seem odd because they are balanced with moderate immersion. The sign of dysregulation is that we lose the capacity to alternate and are stuck in a detached, objectifying state.

Disordered Consciousness and Disordered Sense of Self: The Loss of Complexity and Coherence

I've discussed the immersion-detachment dimension of consciousness first not because it is the most important aspect of the experience of dysregulation, but simply because it served to illustrate moderate and severe types of disordered consciousness. I now discuss additional ways that consciousness becomes disordered. I'll describe how dysregulation results

in a *constriction of consciousness*—a loss of complexity. As consciousness becomes constricted, there is a concomitant sense that the self has
contracted. When dysregulated, there is also a *breakdown of the coherence of consciousness* and a concomitant sense of a disruption of the
coherence of the self.

The Constriction of Consciousness: The Loss of Complexity

Let me begin by reviewing what some of what we've already discussed
about the comings and goings of the complexity of consciousness. Recall
that the development of consciousness begins with a single-level consciousness (primary consciousness) assembled by implicit processes mediated
subcortically by the right brain. The left brain and the prefrontal cortices
have yet to develop. At this point, we are aware of only the present taken in
by global attention. It is comprised of the whole of the perceived world at
that moment with us at the center. We are without reflective processes and
thus responding to objects automatically. When we regress to such states,
our behaviors are scripted by implicit memories that have encoded prior
experiences with objects that are like the object currently being processed.

During the second year, a reflective level is added to consciousness,
and explicit processes begin to develop along with increasingly complex
implicit cognitions. Consciousness becomes exponentially more differentiated and complex. An inner, private space can be conjured—a representational world. An array of complex mental operations begins to form that are
essential for further development and adaptive functioning. We acquire a
temporal context. Verbal-reflective processes allow a secondary processing
of affects. We become able to direct our attention and think deliberately. We
become agents. Mature defenses develop—rationalization, intellectualization, sublimation, and other forms of repression. Analogy and metaphor
become possible expanding and deepening meaning. All of this processing
is disabled, and all of this complexity collapses when we're dysregulated.

As Jackson's theory of neural dissolution proposed (1931a, 1931b),
higher order processes are deactivated when affect is dysregulated. We shift
into a constricted state of consciousness in which we are reduced to simple
phenomenological awareness of ourselves existing in the present responding to objects automatically. We saw this in the extreme in Chapter 2 with
my slip on the stairs.

The experience of this contraction is the inverse of the sense of expansion that comes when affect attunement induces shared states of consciousness (Tronick, 2004; Tronick et al., 1998). Rather, there is a sense of consciousness being cramped and of the self being diminished. No wonder. There has been a collapse of inner space, a loss of capacity for deliberate processing that takes place in it, and a loss all the functionality it supports. In my experience, this sense of constriction occurs in both hyper- and hypo-aroused types of disordered consciousness. However, the constriction occurs in the context of other, very different experiences of being dysregulated. We just saw one of these differences—immersion versus detachment. Let's now look at the breakdown of coherence.

The Breakdown of Coherence: Fragmented-Flooded Versus Empty-Barren

I draw here from one of Grice's maxims (1975) used for scoring the coherence of narratives in response to the Adult Attachment Interview. To fulfill the maxim of quantity, coherence requires that responses to questions supply enough but not too much or too little information. Let's look first at states of consciousness with regard to the problem of too much information. They are generated by over-activated mental processes driven by dysregulated hyper-aroused affect. This is often a chronic problem for those with preoccupied attachment. Such patients report being overwhelmed by thoughts and feelings that surge in, each powerful but fleeting and replaced by the next that may contradict it, or it may be an association that takes one in an entirely different direction. Integrative processes can't keep up. The corresponding experience of the self is of being fragmented and of being "all over the place."

In such states of dysregulated hyper-arousal, thoughts may become distorted in the sense that one aspect becomes overly prominent, while others that should be influential are crowded out. Overwhelmed, patients are unable to reflect on or put events into perspective. One patient referred to his thinking as "scrambled." Another said she felt "like a balloon that you blow up and let go and it darts all over the place." At another point, with a hand choking her neck, she described a sense of being emotionally flooded with thoughts that "zip in and out, first this, then that." and of being unable to pull back and make sense of what's happening.

These are highly charged, unintegrated thoughts, each compelling because of its affective intensity. Each generates a momentary absolute belief and urge to act. Reflective functioning may be compromised to the point where it is simply along for the ride, simply aware of what's happening. Interestingly, some patients are struck by sharp jolts of affect, while others report a numbing. One patient described the latter as generating a "weird kind of distance, as though I don't care even though I'm crying and yelling."

Compare this pandemonium to the slowed and vacuous experience of the moderately dysregulated, hypo-aroused states of consciousness typically associated with avoidant attachment. Whereas hyper-aroused, fragmented states are expressed overtly, for example, in the rapidity of speech and breakdown in syntax, hypo-aroused states are less obvious. They are expressed implicitly by a stillness of the body, including the face, and a flattened vocal tone, all indicative of a hypo-aroused affect state. Such patients report a slowed-down, grayed-out, affectless state accompanied by a sense of mental sluggishness. Associative activity is absent. There is a dulled or even a total absence of felt experience.[7] Whereas the hyper-aroused patient experiences mental hyperactivity and a sense of being overwhelmed, the hypo-aroused patient experiences mental hypo-activity, a sense of thoughts not coming, and a barren inner world. The corresponding experience of the self is that it is deactivated and empty. One patient, experiencing incapacitating hypo-arousal at a social event, reported finding it difficult to process the interactions quickly enough to keep up with conversations and having the sense that his mind was "blank." Note that in both cases there is a loss of agency and a frightening sense of being out of control.

Summary and Conclusion

Being dysregulated and in a disordered state of consciousness is a multi-dimensional experience and qualitatively different depending on whether the dysregulation is hyper- or hypo-aroused. However, both types involve: *the alteration of one's relationship to experience*—being involuntarily immersed in or detached from experience, *the collapse of complexity* largely due to being without reflective capacity, and *the breakdown of coherence*—being overwhelmed by thoughts and feelings and experiencing oneself as fragmented, or being without thoughts and feelings and experiencing oneself as deactivated and empty. Such states of consciousness and concomitant states of the self are markers of dysregulated affect that has

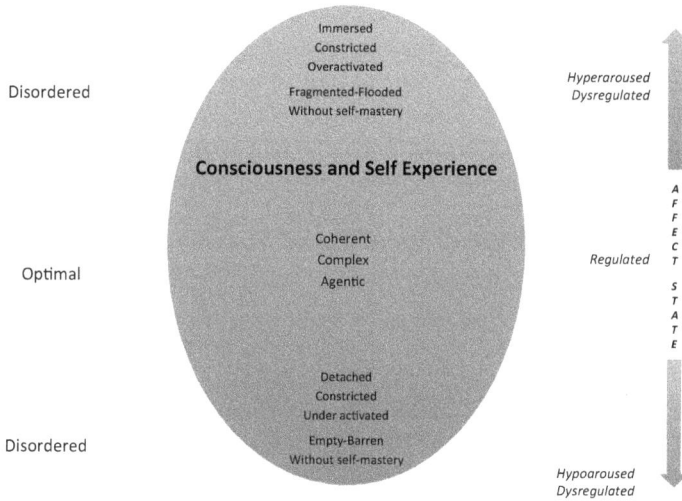

Figure 4.1 Consciousness and Self-Experience Are Affect State Dependent.

disrupted the integrated functioning of neural systems underlying normal waking consciousness (see Figure 4.1).

Notes

1 Note that both single incident trauma and the cumulative trauma of early attachment may result in a post-traumatic disorder marked by both hyper- and hypo-aroused sequelae. Schore (1994) argues that disorganized attachment is the result of a severed autonomic nervous system and thus suffers from severely dysregulated states of both hyper- and hypo-arousal.

2 In neuroimaging studies, Lanius and her colleagues (2007, 2010, 2012) found a subset of patients suffering from an "under-modulated," hyper-aroused type of PTSD (about 70% of their sample). It is associated with low cortical activity and high subcortical activity in response to hearing a transcript of one's trauma story. These were the patients who were vulnerable to flashbacks and other reliving experiences. In the other type of PTSD, an "over-modulated," hypo-aroused type (about 30%), the response was an over-inhibition by cortical structures of subcortically mediated sympathetic arousal. These patients were vulnerable to depersonalization-derealization.

3 Empirical confirmation of this led to a change in the *DSM-5*. PTSD had been understood as a biphasic disorder. That is, it was thought that patients experienced periods of hyper-arousal marked by chronic anxiety, sleep disturbance, hypervigilance, and irritability, alternating with periods of hypo-arousal marked by psychological constriction and social withdrawal.

4   According to the model I'm proposing, they have regressed to a state of primary implicit consciousness versus primary explicit consciousness.
5   Of course, the sequelae of early attachment trauma can also be considered a post-traumatic disorder. It should perhaps be called "ptsd."
6   It should be noted that the trauma of disorganized attachment results in severe dysregulation. This chapter concerns only the more common traumas of structured insecure attachment.
7   This may be due to endogenous opiods, cortical overregulation, or damage to subcortical structures that mediate affective experience.

Bibliography

Ataria, Y. (2014). Acute peritraumatic: In favor of a phenomenological inquiry. *Journal of Trauma and Dissociation, 15*, 332–347.

Breuer, J., & Freud, S. (1955). Studies on hysteria. In J. Strachey (Ed.), *The standard edition of the complete psychological works of Sigmund Freud*. London: Hogarth. (Original work published 1893)

Bromberg, P. (2006). *Awakening the dreamer: Clinical journeys*. Mahwah, NJ: Analytic Press.

Chefetz, R. (2015). *Intensive psychotherapy for persistent dissociative processes.* New York: Norton.

Dell, P. (2009a). The phenomena of pathological dissociation. In P. Dell & J. O'Neil (Eds.), *Dissociation and the dissociative disorders: DSM-V and beyond* (pp. 225–238). New York: Routledge.

Dell, P. (2009b). Understanding dissociation. In P. Dell & J. O'Neil (Eds.), *Dissociation and the dissociative disorders: DSM-V and beyond* (pp. 709–826). New York: Routledge.

Frewen, P., & Lanius, R. (2015). *Healing the traumatized self.* New York: Norton.

Grice, H. P. (1975). Logic and conversation. In P. Cole & J. L. Morgan (Eds.), *Syntax and semantics: Vol. III. Speech acts* (pp. 41–58). New York: Academic Press.

Jackson, J. H. (1931a). *Selected writings of J.H. Jackson. Vol. 1*. London: Hodder and Soughton.

Jackson, J. H. (1931b). *Selected writings of J.H. Jackson. Vol. 2*. London: Hodder and Soughton.

James, W. (1902). *The varieties of religious experience*. New York: Longmans, Green.

Janet, P. (1889). *L'automatisme psychologique: Essai de psychologie experimentale sur les forms inferieures de l'activite humaine*. Paris: Felix Alcan.

Janet, P. (1901). *The mental state of hysterics.* New York: Putnam.

Lanius, R. A., Bluhm, R., & Lanius, U. (2007). Posttraumatic stress disorder symptom provocation and neuroimaging. In E. Vermetten, M. J. Dorahy, & D. Spiegel (Eds.), *Traumatic dissociation: Neurobiology and treatment* (pp. 191–217). Washington, DC: American Psychiatric Press.

Lanius, R. A., Bluhm, R., Lanius, U., & Pain, C. (2006). A review of neuroimaging studies in PTSD: Heterogeneity of response to symptom provocation. *Journal of Psychiatric Research, 40*, 709–729.

Lanius, R. A., Brand, B., Vermetten, E., Frewen, P. A., & Spiegel, D. (2012). The dissociative subtype of posttraumatic stress disorder: Rationale, clinical and neurobiological evidence, and implications. *Depression and Anxiety, 29*, 1–8. doi:10.1002/da.21889

Lanius, R. A., Vermetten, E., Loewenstein, R. J., Brand, B., Schmahl, C., Bremner, J. D., & Spiegel, D. (2010). Emotion modulation in PTSD: Clinical and neurobiological evidence for a dissociative subtype. *American Journal of Psychiatry, 167*, 640–647.

Schore, A. N. (1994). *Affect regulation and the origin of the self: The neurobiology of emotional development.* New York: Norton.

Schore, A. N. (2012). *The science of the art of psychotherapy.* New York: Norton.

Stein, D. J., Koenen, K. C., Friedman, M. J., Hill, E., McLaughlin, K. A., Petukhova, M., et al. (2013). Dissociation in posttraumatic stress disorder: Evidence from the world mental health surveys. *Biological Psychiatry, 73*, 302–312.

Tronick, E. (2004). Why is connection with others so critical? The formation of dyadic states of consciousness and the expansion of individuals' states of consciousness. In E. Tronick (Ed.), *The neurobehavioral and social-emotional development of infants and children* (pp. 476–499). New York: Norton.

Tronick, E., & The Boston Change Process Study Group. (1998). Dyadically expanded states of consciousness and the process of therapeutic change. *Infant Mental Health Journal, 19*(3), 290–299.

Vaitl, D., Birbaumer, N., Gruzelier, J., Jamieson, G. A., Kotchoubey, B., Kübler, A., Lehmann, D., Miltner, W. H. R., Ott, U., Pütz, P., Sammer, G., Strauch, I., Strehl, U., Wackermann, J., & Weiss, T. (2005). Psychobiology of altered states of consciousness. *Psychological Bulletin, 131*(1), 98–127.

Wolf, E. J., Miller, M. W., Reardon, A. F., Ryabchenko, K. A., Castillo, D., & Freund, R. (2012). A latent class analysis of dissociation and posttraumatic stress disorder: Evidence for a dissociative subtype. *Archives of General Psychiatry, 69*(7), 698–705.

Chapter 5

Ken and Barbara

A Clinical Application of the Model

In the previous chapters, I have proposed a model of a mind organized by affect. It is comprised of implicit and explicit processes that operate at primary and reflective levels. Consciousness, with the self at its center, is a late developing feature of this mind. Implicit and explicit processes assemble our states of consciousness and our subjective experience, and they perform core adaptive functions.

We've seen that hyper-arousal activates implicit processes. They are mediated by the right brain. They assemble the present, perform functions in real time, and generate implicit consciousness. Moderate arousal activates explicit processes. They are mediated by the left brain. They process the past and future, generate explicit consciousness, and perform functions prospectively and retroactively. Implicit processes perform the foundational function of the self—the primary regulation of affect. All other functions and adaptive states of consciousness depend on it. When affect is dysregulated, our functioning is impaired and our consciousness becomes disordered.

In this chapter, I illustrate key tenets of this model with clinical examples. The patients I discuss, Ken and Barbara, are composites, or perhaps it would be better to say distillations of an array of patients that I've seen over the years who were suffering with the sequelae of avoidant or preoccupied attachment trauma. Therapeutic events are compressed in my telling. They often happened in bits and pieces with aspects learned implicitly and explicitly over a period of time.

The Ken and Barbara I present here have predecessors. In my previous book, Ken represented an ideal type, rarely found in nature, of a personality structured by an avoidant attachment pattern. Barbara represented an ideal type with a preoccupied attachment pattern. Here too they are archetypes

DOI: 10.4324/9781003266617-6

created for heuristic purposes. Of course, in reality, personality traits don't fall so neatly into place, and it's always interesting to see how patients deviate from type. When thinking of actual patients, we recognize that most have developed several internal working models that are activated in different contexts. It's also important to keep in mind that these are spectrum disorders with varying degrees of severity. The Ken and Barbara I've created manifest moderate to severe degrees of avoidant and preoccupied sequelae.

In my previous book, I focused on Ken and Barbara's regulatory deficits, defensive relational patterns, and their engrained, shame ridden sense of self. We followed them as they went through the Strange Situation and examined the different types of early attachment trauma they had incurred. I then discussed the sequelae of such trauma: autonomic biases toward hyper- or hypo-arousal and deficiencies in regulating affect that resulted in dysregulation-dissociation at low levels of stress. We also saw that such early attachment trauma is essentially a shame trauma. It left Ken and Barbara with narcissistic personality disorders and unable to process shame. As a result, unconscious shame permeated their personalities and they suffered from developmental arrests. Finally, we saw that the sequelae of such trauma took very different forms, one supported by hyper-arousal and the other supported by hypo-arousal.

Ken and Barbara represent dramatically different types of insecure attachment. At the bottom of their differences is their autonomic bias. Recall that arousal biases are marked by one's set point and response to stress. Ken is biased toward hypo-arousal, and Barbara toward hyper-arousal. Such biases support contrasting relational strategies—different ways of being in relationships developed to defend against a repetition of their trauma. The hypo-aroused temperment that is the keystone of avoidant attachment supports a deactivated, introverted, socially withdrawn, passive, overaccommodating, deflated personality. It defends against anticipated rejection and fear of being overwhelmed by affect. The hyper-arousal that is hallmark of preoccupied attachment supports a hyper-activated, extroverted, highly social, often controlling, inflated personality. It defends against anticipated abandonment and fear of hypo-aroused affect states.

I'll review some of this when I reintroduce Ken and Barbara below. However, in my depiction of them, this time I will focus on the concerns of this book. We will look at the states of consciousness toward which they are inclined. They live in different worlds and are disposed to different ways of being in them. I will also focus on how Ken and Barbara's deficiencies in the regulation of affect effect their capacities for intersubjectivity, agency, and self-generation.

Ken

Ken, middle-aged, came to therapy at the insistence of his wife (Janet) who was at her wits end and was threatening to leave the marriage. *She says I'm always criticizing her.* I asked if it were true. *Not really. I mean, she can't accept advice. It wouldn't be a problem if she could deal with it.* In a subsequent session he offered, *Janet says to tell you I'm never "present."* (Gesturing scare quotes.) *She's right about that. I'm often thinking about something else when she's talking.* Then, several sessions later… *She's* always *complaining about our lack of "closeness," whatever she means by that.* What do you think she means? *I don't know. We stopped having sex a long time ago. Why would I want to? She's always on my case.* (Let's leave aside that Janet's complaint was that he was always criticizing her and that there may be a problem of mutual toxic shaming going on. In my experience, it is a common problem in insecure relationships.) I asked what he wanted to get out of therapy. *I don't want my marriage to end. She's always threatening to leave.*

I was struck by the fact that Ken would sometimes giggle while telling me of the problems in his marriage. At first, I thought that he was laughing contemptuously at Janet and her concerns. It turned out that the giggle was involuntary, an automatism. *It's some kind of nervous laughter that I've had forever. It's embarrassing. I can control it most of the time.* It occurred when he introduced a stressful topic and masked his actual feelings about it. In this case, we found that it did include a measure of defensive contempt but also a mixture of fear and shame about the incident he was describing.

Ken was avoidantly attached. It was not hard to sense that he had a parasympathetic autonomic bias. Especially at first, before he and I had settled in, he talked in a measured monotone, his body stilled, his face impassive. Note that in telling me of why he came to therapy there was no mention of inner states. Indeed, he was without much ability to read his own or other's affect states. He was often unaware of his own subjective experience and with little capacity for intersubjective relating. He had poor socioemotional intelligence and limited understanding of how the mind works or of the role of affect in mental life.

Ken relied on autoregulation. He was disinclined to seek connection and dyadic regulation; indeed, he shied away from it. Typical of those with avoidant attachment, he was afraid of being overwhelmed by affect. He avoided even the pleasurable hyper-arousal and felt sense connection that attunement engenders. Moreover, for Ken, revealing his vulnerabilities came with the expectation of being shamed.

In keeping with this, I sensed a social awkwardness and remoteness in Ken and came to find that he was acutely aware of it. *I can be social, but it always feels stilted, and it is. At parties, even at work events, no one speaks to me for long.* Ken's emotional detachment and social anxiety were sequelae of dismissive attachment trauma, its damage to the limbic-autonomic system, and the character defenses he adopted to avoid more of the same. He had difficulty modulating the intensity of hyper-arousal resulting in his core fear of being overwhelmed by affect. His distancing relational moves, such as not making eye contact and pre-empting or abbreviating shared affect states, were also defensive. They were implemented to guard against overwhelming hyper-arousal.

Janet organized their social life. They go on vacations and play cards with a variety of other couples, and they are members of a pool club where, during summers, they hang out with friends. Ken told me that he tags along with her on weekends, but *It's boring. Small talk. I sneak off and read whenever I can. I'm sort of a loner. I mean not really a loner. I have friends but I never had a real friend. I don't keep in touch with anyone I grew up with or went to college with. The last thing I want is to be on Facebook.*

Life was little better at work, a large NYC law firm. As in his marriage, here too Ken endured. He found the work tedious and disliked the relentless pressure to meet deadlines and produce billable hours. He particularly disliked the internal politics which, unsurprisingly given his deficient socio-emotional intelligence, he was poor at navigating. He no longer hoped to make partner, but *I've carved out a niche for myself. It's secure, pays decently. I'm OK with it.*

Unaware of the extent to which his sense of inferiority and insufficient self-respect had played a role in his life, Ken had never let himself aspire to much and kept his expectations low. Discovering the pervasive influence of shame in his mental economy was a revelation. *Now I realize that it was always there. I mean I always knew it but somehow didn't know it. It's all over the place.* Of course, knowing about it is one thing, and changing the myriad of scripted, personality traits that had developed from his core sense of not being valued is another. A considerable amount of his treatment was devoted to working this through. Ken felt that the change in his sense of self was the most important thing he'd acquired from therapy.

Having sensed Ken's downregulated temperament early on, I wasn't surprised to find that he was left brain dominant. His inattention to affect states, processed in the right brain, had also suggested left brain dominance. Additionally, the left brain's objectification of others helped explain his emotional distance that was so palpable to Janet and to himself. I understood early on that activating the right brain would be a treatment goal, and that the vitality in working with him would, at least initially, originate with me.

At one point, Ken began to talk about fights he had with Janet during which he would lose control and fly into a rage, never physical violence but in-your-face-screaming However, most commonly, when stressed, he became hypo-aroused, emotionally detached, and submissive. *When she gets crazy on me, I shut down. Thinking about it now, I'm really on autopilot, just going through the motions. I apologize, take the blame, just trying to get her to calm her down.* In the first instance, when his defenses against anger failed, we see the difficulty Ken has modulating the intensity of hyper-arousal. He was unable to turn anger into adaptive assertiveness. In the second instance, when frightened, Ken "shut down" became detached and submissive. Here we see how hypo-arousal serves him defensively but note that he's lost control of himself here as well. He's dysregulated and automatized, enacting scripted accommodating responses.

Ken was not without insights, but rather he tended not to follow up by reflecting on them and without enough socio-emotional intelligence to think about them productively. At one point, he found the courage to say, out loud, *Janet says I don't have any feelings. Sometimes I'm afraid she's right.* He had this thought himself over the years, been ashamed of it, and suppressed it without further processing. *It's another one of those things I knew and didn't know at the same time.* Ken's treatment, especially in the beginning, involved a considerable amount of emotional education, naming affects, analyzing defenses against them, exploring the affective dynamics between him and Janet, etc. Perhaps surprisingly, Ken was excited by this aspect of his treatment. The hope is that with time and use these explicit knowings will become implicit knowings available to him in real time. But helping Ken tolerate and use affects adaptively must go on at the implicit level as well. The cognitive grasp provided by words helps, but the experience of regulating them implicitly is fundamental, first dyadically with me, and then automatically by himself. I'll come back to this below.

Ken's treatment also focused on his shame-ridden sense of himself and its implicit expression in his life. It was enacted in his submissiveness, and the negative expectations associated with it underlay his social anxiety. Changes at this implicit level are achieved most efficiently through the implicit therapeutic relationship. Here's an example, a moment in which we connected. I believe it increased his capacity to process shame and put a dent in his low self-esteem.

Ken giggled while telling me of his alexithymia. By this time we had established that it was an automatism triggered by affects he wasn't able to regulate, in this case the shame of being without feelings. He was embarrassed about the nervous giggle which added to his woes. I moved to regulate him interactively, to help him manage the stress. At one point this happened.

As he was telling me about not having feelings, and while he was giggling uncomfortably, I looked at him with a knowing sympathetic smile that by this time conveyed something like "I understand what's happening. I know you're struggling. I'm not judging you." I'm not sure, but in retrospect there may have also been a twinkle in my expression, some indication that I found some humor in the absurdity of giggling in the midst of such distress. Or maybe it came from him. In any case, we both broke into laughter, caught up in the relief it provided. We let the laughter last as long as it lasted. It was fun. Talking about it later he teared up.

Such therapeutic moments, mediated by implicit communications and made up of interactive regulation of shame and shared joy, are usually less obvious. Most are less intense and go unnoticed, simply part of the warp and woof of the implicit therapeutic relationship that encode experiences of secure attachment. I should mention that over the course of therapy Ken's nervous giggle almost disappeared, suggesting an increased capacity to modulate the intensity of stressful affects. When it did show up, he would suppress it, stick up a finger telling me to give him a moment. A twinkle in his eye and a hint of a smile suggested to me that he was proud of being able to manage the stress. Perhaps it was also that he and I had fond memories of laughing at it. In either case, it offset the distress of the negative affects he was dealing with and perhaps helped establish positive expectations.

Talking about the incident later, Ken told me that he realized that one of the reasons he enjoyed it was because he thought that laughing with one's therapist was against the rules. Not long after telling me this, he called me Dan rather than Dr. Hill. I think it caught us both by surprise. We never spoke about it, however, in the moment he made it clear that he enjoyed it. I thought it had a devilish quality to it and I made it clear that I was fine with it. Actually, I was pleased. It was spontaneous. I took it to be indicative of Ken's increasingly secure sense of himself and increasing capacity for spontaneity and self-assertion.

To this point, I have focused on the effects of Ken's autonomic bias on his regulatory and relational patterns. Let's now look at how hypo-arousal organizes his states of consciousness and how his regulatory difficulties interfere with his capacity for intersubjectivity, agency, and self-generation. I'll start with what I touched on briefly above: his left brain dominance and the explicit consciousness it constructs.

Ken's left brain dominance delimited his experience of the world, his way of thinking about it, and his way of being in it. At one point in college, hearing others talking about a work of fiction that had been assigned, he realized that, unlike them, he did not picture the scene he'd been reading about. As a result, *I never really get into it like they do. I'd power through it reading for what I might need to pass the test, but that's it.* Ken seemed to have been reading with his left brain only. The picturing required to bring the book to life requires the right brain and the affect that comes with it. This was also true when others spoke of personal experiences. He didn't *experience* the events he read or was told about. Ken lived, much of the time, in an abstracted world of words with little appreciation of the inner life behind them. He lived on the surface.

Picturing what he read and what others said became a project of Ken's. This was his own invention. For my part, I found myself using metaphors more than usual, or perhaps I was simply more aware of my use of them, but in either case I seem to have joined his project of activating his right brain. (Recall that metaphors are processed in the right brain.) When a metaphor was introduced, we often took unstated delight in using it. There was an element of play in passing it back and forth and stretching it. The moderate shared joy served as a counterbalance to the negative material we were discussing, and it generated an emotional bond, a sense of usness. There was an intimacy to it. The use of metaphor in this way provided emotional and representational attunement and, I could tell, generated the dyadically expanded states of consciousness and the openness and receptivity that come with them. They were often high points of sessions.

At one point, Ken realized that he didn't believe, in the sense that he didn't experience it as real, that Janet would end the marriage. This in spite of the fact that she hadn't wavered from her position since she first told him several months earlier. Such moderately derealized states were not uncommon for Ken, especially in social situations. In a similar vein, he once told me that sometimes when he's telling me of an incident in his marriage, he feels like he's telling me about something he dreamt.

Ken had a low tolerance for stress and was frequently moderately dysregulated and thus frequently in moderately disordered states of consciousness. Note that, with regard to Janet's intention to end the marriage, his failure to really realize what was happening wasn't a result of denial. The affect was dissociated and simply hadn't hit him—yet. The blow landed inadvertently when, without any great therapeutic intention, I referred to the situation as Janet "having a foot out the door." The metaphor, a picture, activated his right brain and the affect (fear) that came with it. I saw the blood drain from Ken's face. He was momentarily speechless and started to tear up. I stayed steady, keeping him steady. Now that he'd experienced the affect, Janet's intentions became real.

Here are two other incidents in which Ken's state of consciousness was moderately disordered. There was an episode at work, in which he was scared that a mistake he'd made would be exposed. An alarming email needed to be responded to immediately, which he did. He later realized that he hadn't really processed much of the frightening email, and that he couldn't remember fully what he'd said in response. *I functioned somehow, but on autopilot or something. I didn't really take in the email. When I think about it now, I just jumped around in it. Everything was hazy. If you'd given me a test on it, I would have gotten a "C –."* Ken was in a dysregulated, hypo-aroused constricted state of consciousness. Cognitive systems were barely available, rendering him unable to fully process the very stuff he needed to process. I saw more severe versions of this in treatment. Especially in the early stage, Ken would begin sessions with a prepared topic and then run out of things to say. He would sit silently, looking at me with a sad, embarrassed face. I understood this as him "shutting down" in response to stress, his spontaneous thoughts not coming to him. I would try to help him out. After a while I could do this effectively with just a look of understanding, a "don't worry about it" shrug, a sympathetic smile and letting him deal with it. Sometimes I encouraged him verbally saying in a moderately upbeat tone, "Try to say what's going through your mind" adding something like "Easy for me to say." I wanted to connect with and enliven him to activate his right brain.

Ken's left brain dominance and life in the explicit lane played an important role in his Janet's complaint that he was constantly criticizing her and often wasn't present. She spoke in a highly associative style. *Drives me nuts. She takes forever to get to the point. Other times she makes her point up front and then goes on and on about it off in all different directions.* This, as opposed to Ken's linear, convergent, get-to-the-point way of processing material — good for practicing the law. Ken dealt with his frustration, in typical avoidant fashion, by turning his attention elsewhere. Before he knew it, he would find himself thinking about something else. His narrow focus was also a problem. (Recall that the left brain mediates focal attention.) For his wife, the issue at hand had many tributaries feeding in and out of it. Finally, listening with the left brain is not receptive. Whereas the right brain listens in order to take it all in as it is, the left brain analyzes, looks for loopholes, and is skeptical. Ken's overriding concern with coherence kept him alert to assumptions, ambiguities, inconsistencies, etc. If I made an analogy, the gist of which made my point, Ken picked at a part of it that didn't quite fit.

Let me end this section with a discussion of how Ken's rather severe emotional detachment not only dictated a top-down approach in the early stages of treatment but also provided therapeutic opportunities. I sensed early on that I could be straightforward with him. Indeed, he appreciated explicit directness. However, given his avoidance of stressful material and impoverished capacity for growth-oriented introspection, there was a concern about how much of what we discussed would be chewed on and digested. It's not only that Ken didn't listen openly and associatively and often doesn't experience the affect associated with what is being said, he also didn't spend time thinking about what he encountered. My concern was that he registered what I said, albeit faintly, and then went about the business of keeping his attention diverted, successfully defending against further processing the disturbing material. Here's an example of using bluntness to get through to him, dysregulating him, of and then of interactively reregulating him. Therapeutically, it provides him with the experience of interactive regulation, an intimate act that is not what he grew up with. I would only be this blunt with severe avoidants and only after trust in my nurturant intentions had been well established. I offer it to illustrate a variety of issues.

Recall that Ken said that his goal in therapy was to save his marriage. He repeated it a while later, *I really don't want to be back out there on my own.*

This time, with a gentle firmness but nevertheless anxious about the shame I was about to induce, I said something that I'd thought of before but hesitated to say—that I suspected that what Janet might most appreciate was the feeling that he didn't want to keep hurting her. Reconstructing this moment later, I realized I saw the shame hit him and had spontaneously moved in to connect with him and modulate its intensity. At the same time, I added what I thought to be true, that his fear of Janet leaving crowded out his concern for her well-being. Ideally, this would be a step toward increased tolerance for shame and increased capacity to use it constructively, in this case, to begin to come to grips with his empathic failures and egocentrism.

It was also a moment in which he could see that although it wasn't his intention to hurt Janet, that was the effect of his need to correct her. Her experience of being criticized hadn't been considered, not in real time nor reflectively. He didn't tend to see into her and lacked the intuitive understanding of emotional life that would inform his empathy. For him, the problem is that she can't accept criticism which he feels is good advice. He's only aware of her anger and not of the shame he induced behind it. While my intervention is an example of how we induce tolerable shame in the service of development, my starting point was that Ken's emotional detachment, his thick skin, allowed, and perhaps required, a therapeutic frankness.

We've been discussing how the sequelae of avoidant trauma manifested in Ken's regulatory and relational patterns and in disordered states of consciousness. Let's now discuss how they interfere with his capacity to perform fundamental adaptive functions.

We've seen that intersubjectivity, agency, and self-generation all depend on the regulation of affect. We've also seen that Ken and Barbara are both deficient in this foundational function. However, they have opposite autonomic biases, different kinds of regulatory problems, and different kinds of problems with each of these self-functions. I'll continue here with examples of how these sequelae of avoidant trauma impede Ken's functioning. I'll discuss Barbara's difficulties in the next section.

Intersubjectivity

While both Barbara and Ken have suffered damage to the limbic-autonomic system, the trauma to Ken's is earlier and thus more far-reaching. It left him with a narrow range of downregulated affects that he is able to regulate and in which he dwells. Most fundamentally for intersubjectivity, the cumulative effects of dismissal on his limbic-autonomic system left him deficient in the ability to detect and assess his own or other's affect states. He had little capacity for real-time, primary intersubjectivity.

The resulting deficiency in real-time socio-emotional navigation contributed significantly to Ken's social anxiety. He is often moderately dysregulated in social situations, behaviorally inhibited and in a dissociated-detached state of consciousness. *It's ok if I'm with a bunch of people I work with every day because we can talk work stuff, but sometimes, like at parties it can get bad. I feel removed, sometimes weirdly removed. I just go stand with groups listening, feeling I don't fit in and very self-conscious. Sometimes I say something but usually they barely know I'm there.*

He was also deficient in reflective intersubjectivity. Not only did he lack an implicit-intuitive understanding of emotional life that sets the stage for verbal-reflective intersubjectivity, his lack of exposure to mind-talk in his family left him deficient in the language of emotion and without a disposition to think about it let alone discuss it with others.

Ken's deficient intersubjective capacities were most problematic at home where his inability to connect emotionally or talk about what was going on had a powerful effect on Janet. Unfortunately, her quickness to anger and intersubjective dependency exacerbated Ken's deficiencies and drove him further away. *She's so needy. Sometimes I make up things to do just so I can be by myself. Either she's angry at me or going on about things I couldn't care less about.* But it is not only Ken's avoidance of Janet's anger, nor his lack of interest in her socio-emotional concerns, nor in his aversion to her need for contact that were a problem.

Ken's need for distance in intimate relationships originated in his fear of being overwhelmed by affect. He told me of the following incident that occurred with his college girlfriend. *I had this weird experience. We were talking and it got really intense. I felt so close to her that I suddenly felt like I was going to melt. Literally. Melt. It was terrifying. I still shudder when I think of it.* While this story epitomizes Ken's fear of being overwhelmed by powerful affects, he shied away even from the amplified affect generated by the run-of-the-mill affect attunement—the coin of the realm in attachment relationships. He shied away from eye contact and simultaneously shared affect states.

With regard to Ken's fear of melting, whatever else being in-love may be, it is an intensely hyper-aroused state that activates the right brain, softens and opens us, puts us deeply in the moment, and generates a sense of merger. It apparently overwhelmed Ken who experienced a terrifying sense of self-dissolution. Ken's avoidance of connection was one of Janet's primary distresses. *Her shrink said I was "afraid of intimacy."* (again the scare quotes). We came to understand that he was indeed afraid of intimacy, afraid of being overwhelmed by the intense affect it generates, and ultimately afraid of melting. On top of this, once Ken's attachment patterns kicked in, the relationship developed a core conflict. Ken looked down on, actually was disgusted by Janet's need for dyadic regulation. *She's so needy. It really turns me off.* And, of course, chronic dismissal had left him ill-disposed to seeking dyadic regulation himself, further frustrating Janet's need for emotional connection.

Agency: Recall that agency is the capacity to act intentionally and to act or not act. First and foremost, it requires the regulation of the affect. This allows the assessment of the affect behind the intention, allows for deciding whether to act or not, and enables mastery over the action or inaction it urges. Easily dysregulated and without access to the affect, Ken lacked this flexibility. When stressed, his parasympathetic bias deactivated him. Most commonly, the failure to act agentically was due to involuntary *inaction*. However his deficient capacity to regulate hyperarousal, to modulate the intensity of upregulated affects he sometimes found himself *acting* involuntarily.

Rather than a balanced autonomic system that would allow him to either accommodate *or* assimilate the situation at hand, Ken's parasympathetic bias disposed him toward accommodation. For example, he had adjusted to his failure to make partner with notable ease and without seeking alternative possibilities *I get it. They want folks who are going to bring in new business or who can manage a staff. I'm OK with it. The money's not bad.* As in his marriage, Ken dealt with the stresses at work by enduring stoically, in this case by dissociating; by not experiencing the disappointment and humiliation and pressing-on undaunted. Of course, such coping comes at a price. While in some ways this may look like an adaptive adjustment to the reality of his limitations and an ability to accept disappointment, Ken kept his expectations low and was underrealized. He did not see himself as valued or entitled, which was enacted in his overly accommodating style. The shame around his passivity was repressed, to wit he once flew into a rage when Janet implied that he was passive.

Ken's difficulties regulating hyper-aroused affects also interfered with his capacity for agency. This time the problem was involuntary actions. He could lose his temper easily and fly into a rage. In positive states of hyper-arousal, he could become exhibitionistic. At the same time, his defenses against his anger also interfered with acting agentically. He would dissociate or repress it, rather than modulating it and converting it to self-assertion.

Let me end this discussion of Ken's deficiencies regarding agency with a therapeutic success. It had to do with his improved tolerance for stressful affects and increased control over his attention, an example of agentic thinking. *I was in the shower this morning and had this fleeting thought of a fight Janet and I had yesterday. Then came a thought of you and then, believe it or not, I actually thought about the fight!* (Laughing). *I really liked being able to do that. I even thought that I would tell you about it, get your take on it.* Ken took pride in and experienced a sense of mastery at being able to direct his attention toward rather than away from a stressful issue. As an aside, note that Ken's pride is bringing the vitality to our interaction. And finally, the icing on the cake, he wanted to get my take on the fight with Janet. He was seeking dyadic processing.

Self-Generation: Recall that, as with the other functions we've been discussing, self-generation has primary and secondary systems. In this case, the primary system is dyadic. Mother-infant attunement generates shared, expanded states of consciousness that increase complexity and coherence. The secondary system is autonomous—the processing of one's stream of consciousness—James's "duplex self." Like so much else, its development depends on the mother's capacity for attunement. Recall that, much as we do when listening to our patients, she takes a background, observing and resonating role as the child speaks the thoughts that come to mind. She will be internalized as the "I" of the child's duplex self, observing its stream of consciousness, experienced as "me." The dyadic process becomes autonomous. The mature process involves implicit and explicit processing of one's stream of consciousness, working in tandem to increase the complexity and coherence of the self.

Ken's duplex self was underdeveloped and often impeded by his difficulty processing the stressful emotions accompanying the thoughts coming to mind. His early attachment trauma left him vulnerable to dysregulation-dissociation at low levels of stress and unable to process shame and use it productively for self-correction and growth. Ken's capacity to develop was underdeveloped.

Of course, we are privy only to our own duplex self. I can only speculate about Ken's. However, in working with him, I attempted to turn his attention to the spontaneous thoughts that came to mind while staying connected to him shoring him up against the stress. I draw my speculations from what happened when I did this.

Ken's deficient capacity for self-generation begins with his lack of experience with dyadic self-generation. His history of chronic dismissal in the early attachment relationship left him with expectations of being shamed when seeking connection. Additionally, his lack of sufficient positive experience with attunement left him without the disposition and without the relational moves to engage in it. Finally, the imprint of shame at his core left him with an aversion to the sense of recognition that comes with attunement. Also, I wonder how frequently or effectively his downregulated, disinclined-to-play mother joined him in the original play space and how robust the subsequent development of duplex self was. How curious was she to find out what his thoughts were in response to the issue at hand?

Perhaps the most pervasive impediment to Ken's productive use of his capacity to process his stream of consciousness is that when it comes to processing stressful material, Ken's avoidant defenses are activated. He minimizes the problem and keeps his attention away from it. In our first session, I asked what he thought about Janet's complaints and what he thought about the relationship. *I don't know. To tell you the truth, I really don't think about it much. I mean, when I'm around her she can barely talk about anything else, so, you know... but I'm not obsessed with it the way she is. I think about it when she brings it up.*

Finally, concerning impediments to Ken's self-generation, he not only lacked an intuitive understanding of the mind, but because his family did not engage in mind talk, he lacked the mentalizing capacities that could make sense of it through verbal-reflective processing. Ken's treatment involved considerable explicit emotional education that would not only serve to help him mentalize, but will hopefully become implicit, known to him intuitively, and enabling him to better navigate the socio-emotional environment in real time.

Let's now move on to Barbara, her regulatory weaknesses, disordered states of consciousness, and her difficulties with intersubjectivity, agency and self-generation.

Barbara

Barbara, 38 years old, highly engaging, working as a doctor in an emergency room of a large NYC hospital, had recently married Peter who had a 15-year-old daughter. This is what brought her to therapy. *She's a perfectly nice kid, but she keeps me at arm's length. I'm always trying to get her to like me, to confide in me, to go shopping together, whatever. I used to buy her things I knew she'd like. That went nowhere, probably made it worse. I know I should back off but it's just natural for me, just what I do. Anyway, I'm afraid if I don't get her to like me, it will come between me and Peter. It's happening already. He's very devoted to her.* And then, without skipping a beat... *When Peter isn't around, she stays in her room. She knows it gets to me. She can be a real little bitch. Thankfully, she's with his ex every other week. When she's around everything's different. I can't believe I feel threatened by her. I know it's ridiculous, but there are moments when it gets to me. She's really not a bad kid. She's an adolescent. What do you want?*

Barbara went on to tell me that these kinds of "dramas" have always plagued her. *I'm a mess. There's always a drama going on with Peter or a friend or even at work. I can't get them out of my head. I have to get rid of them. It's been like this my whole life. My mother and I are always at each other. It probably started there.... I mean, maybe it's me, but really, my friends are disappointing. I do so much for them. It's hurtful and infuriating, and I'm always thinking about whether I should say something or am making too much of it.*

You get the idea. Whereas Ken's inner world was hypoactive, and he shied away from thinking about what was going on in himself or in others, Barbara's inner world was hyperactive, and she spent far more time immersed in her dramas than she would have liked. She had considerable strengths. She was alert to, one might say hyperalert to her own and others' inner states and had considerable emotional intelligence, keystones of intersubjectivity. At the same time, she was plagued by ambivalence and misattributions. Did Peter's daughter really intend to hurt her by going to her room? She did not consider the possibility that she wanted privacy or perhaps to escape Barbara's need for connection? Such pre-mentalizing modes of understanding impeded her capacity to navigate socio-emotional life. In this case, we see teleological reasoning. For Barbara, the outcome, her hurt feelings, was indicative of Peter's daughter's intention. It's worth mentioning that, until I pointed it out, Barbara didn't realize that she had made an interpretation.

Note also the abrupt switch to "She can be a real little bitch." Chronic unrepaired ruptures and episodes of virulent shaming left Barbara without the capacity to modulate and process shame. She bypassed it with anger. We came to realize that the dramas that plagued her the most, that she "had to get rid of," were those in which she felt shamed. *These* wrongs needed to be righted! Her narcissistic equilibrium had to be restored, often with vengeful fantasies.

In her last year of medical school, Barbara fell in love, married, and divorced by the end of the summer. *He was terrible. And he left me! Said I was suffocating him. I get that, but really, he couldn't love anyone. I knew that before I married him.* She had several serious relationships during the next decade, but none of them worked out. However, during this period, she had made good use of therapy. Peter was different, and she appreciated it. *I know I can be a lot. He's unfazed by it. He's patient and loving. Really helps me when I get nuts. And he makes me feel good about myself. It's been great. Finally! I was losing hope of ever being in a good relationship.* She had wanted to have children when she was younger but then decided not to. *I'm afraid that I'd be like my mother. I know I would.*

Barbara had never known her father. He died when she was an infant. Like her, her mother was "a lot." She had been a college athlete and was heavily invested in Barbara becoming one as well. *I've always known that sports were the way to her heart. But she was relentless about everything, commenting on what I wore, my makeup, my friends, on being in shape. Even when she didn't say anything, I knew what she was thinking. Once, in a fight, we both broke down crying and I pleaded with her to leave me alone. She said she couldn't, that she loved me too much.*

The pressure to please her mother and their enmeshment were likely factors in an eating disorder that developed in high school and was successfully treated. During this same period, in spite of considerable success, Barbara stopped playing sports entirely. Her mother accused her of quitting to spite her (not entirely untrue) and insisted that it was self-destructive (entirely untrue). *She's always so sure of herself it was hard not to believe her. Even when I knew that she was just being mean, I'd believe her. It's better now but she can still get to me.*

As you've probably already gathered, Barbara had a preoccupied attachment pattern, the sequelae of parenting that was often empathically responsive to her but was inconsistent and often replaced by intrusion. The inconsistency left her with a core fear of abandonment. By intrusions I'm referring to moments in which her mother's needs took precedence over Barbara's. We see this dynamic writ large in her mother's determination that she be an athlete, in her use of Barbara as a narcissistic object. There had also been virulent shaming when her mother became dysregulated and attacked her. It was a highly ambivalent and fraught relationship that left Barbara with a hyper-aroused autonomic bias. As expected, she was right brain dominant.

Barbara was gregarious, with many friends and frenemies. She loved to throw parties and did so at the drop of a hat. During the course of her therapy, she began to see herself as driven by her need to be liked by everyone and anyone. In attachment relationships, which she also formed at the drop of a hat, she was the caretaker. The role was mediated by varying measures of genuine empathy and misattribution but was always an effort to make herself "crucial" (her word) and served as a defense against anticipated abandonment. At one point, while discovering the extent to which compulsive caretaking played a role in her relationships, Barbara said *It's exhausting and I always end up disappointed and resenting it. Half the time I'm taking care of someone before I know it.* She was very proud of being able to give this strategy up and be in more varied and mutual relationships.

Barbara's compulsive caretaking was often experienced as, and, indeed, was often was an effort to control the other person. It was obvious to her that caretaking had developed in response to her fear of being abandoned. She was acutely aware of her mother's needs and of the pressure to meet then. And she was horrified that she had so many of her mother's characteristics. Along with her overdependence on dyadic regulation, this was a factor in why it was not only her first husband who found Barbara suffocating.

Unlike Ken, Barbara was eager to sort out her inner world. Not only did she process it with friends, she turned to therapy when her eating disorder developed in high school, then again during the period when one relationship after another failed, and again briefly when she decided not to have children. Unlike Ken, Barbara was acutely aware of her own and others' inner states, often to a fault. Her heightened subject consciousness was a result of right brain dominance. Awareness of one's own and others' subjective experience is, of course, desirable, however, ideally the awareness is sometimes in the foreground and sometimes in the background. For Barbara, it was stuck in the foreground, with an anxious, hyper-vigilant eye peeled for signs of trouble. (Recall that the right brain mediates global attention and is ever vigilant for signs of danger.) On top of this, she often misinterpreted other's experience, perhaps especially when she imagined what they were thinking about her. *One of the best things I ever heard was a joke that ended with "They're probably not thinking about you at all."*

Whereas Ken had to make an effort to turn his attention toward stressful topics, Barbara couldn't keep hers away from them. Unlike Ken, whose affective experience was dulled or nonexistent and whose inner world was pedestrian and sometimes empty, Barbara's inner world was action packed. Her emotions were powerfully experienced, often conflicting, frequently with sharp edges, and always hard to tamp down. She was heavily dependent on dyadic regulation, but, if therapy was any indication, she often used it for catharsis rather than for productive exploration of the issues at hand. Once this was pointed out to her, she quickly shifted to a more reflective mode. She was highly motivated and capable in this way, in applying what she'd learned in therapy.

Barbara's enthusiasm for and facility in exploring her inner world was striking and made for an efficient therapy. She was eager to reveal and discuss her problems. However, as we saw above, when stressed she tended toward hyper-aroused dysregulation and regressed to pre-mentalizing modes of interpreting others' intentions. Also, and typical of those with a hyper-aroused autonomic bias, she often defended with projection, especially the projection of blame as a defense against shame. This, mixed with pre-mentalizing modes of thought, made for her frequent misattributions.

Barbara was subject to being dramatically different in different affect states. *When I'm with my friends being the life of the party, I really think I'm terrific.* At other times, she felt herself to be …*a failure in every way. I hate myself.* My understanding of this lack of self-constancy is that the strength of her positive or negative affects crowds out any other possibilities. She believes absolutely "I'm terrific" and she believes absolutely "I'm hateful" when each is activated. She's in a hyper-aroused right brain-dominant state, pressed up against the present, without access to reflective processes and the panoramic perspective that comes with them.

None of these states lasted long for Barbara. When she told me she was a mess, she was referring to this mess. *I'm all over the place.* And it could turn on a dime. Interestingly, whereas Ken's experience of therapy was that he had come to life, that he had developed a self, Barbara experienced a sense that she had become whole. As she acquired a greater capacity to modulate the intensity of her affects and stay regulated, reflective capacities were increasingly available enabling the integration of the disparate experiences she had of herself. She may have also developed an implicit awareness, available to her in real time, that affects generate *passing* states of consciousness.

Let me end this discussion with some examples of how Barbara's states of consciousness were affected by the strength of her affect states and her right brain dominance. Let's look at her state of consciousness when a "drama" was going on. Especially in the beginning of therapy, Barbara often talked about fights she had with her mother. Frequently, as she was starting to give me a verbatim account what happened, I would become confused and find it difficult to follow what had occurred and who had said what to whom. She and I reconstructed what happened to her at such moments. She would begin to speak very quickly, a jumble of fragments of sentences. She was trying to keep up with her thoughts as they appeared too quickly for her to manage verbally. For me it was a blur.

Then the next thing I knew, her telling of the fight had switched from the past to the present. That is, suddenly, Barbara was no longer telling me about what *had* happened. Rather, she was reenacting her part in the present. She had become deeply absorbed into the memory of the fight and was attacking her mother in the first person. *The only person you care about it you!* Don't get me wrong. She hadn't lost touch with reality, or rather, it would be more accurate to say she had allowed herself to do so, indulging in the pleasures of venting—and there was this as well.

It took me a couple of times to realize that she was not reenacting what she had actually said to her mother but rather what she would have liked to have said. *All you ever cared about was sports. You're unbelievable. Do you have any idea what a selfish bitch you are. You couldn't have cared less about whether I was happy or not. I've been recovering from you my entire life!!* My understanding of this is that as she was telling me about the fight, she became increasingly hyperactivated and immersed in a revenge fantasy, a highly gratifying fantasy of turning the tables on her mother. In the fantasy, her mother would be shamed, and Barbara was triumphant—a righting of the wrong in the service of her narcissistic equilibrium. My presence had faded into the background.

Again, this was something Barbara *allowed* herself to do with me. Sometimes she would even ask me permission, and as she was gearing up, there would be a rapid fire, *Just let me get through this,* and then at the end, she would thank me for letting her vent. These were the kind of "dramas" she wanted to "get rid of." She would go in and out of such fantasies throughout the day and had difficulty recovering from them. *If I speak with my mother when I'm caught up in this stuff, we're definitely going to have a fight.*

Of course, the real fights never lived up to the fantasy. Even after Barbara was able to better modulate her anger toward her mother, productive discussions were never within reach. Like Barbara, her mother had little tolerance for shame and, rather than using it for self-correction, she would become enraged at Barbara for inducing it. Also, being better able to modulate her anger in general did not mean that she was always able to regulate it with her mother. She used to joke that when she could do this, she was ready to end therapy. She did master this, most of the time.

Let me add one more thing about Barbara's states of consciousness. As you may already have imagined, in stark contrast to Ken's grayed out inner world, Barbara's was vivid, so vivid that experiences imagined there may be confused with memories of actual happenings. For example, she might introduce a topic with a rapid, sotto voce introduction. *We've talked about this.* Or *You know this ...* and then tell me something I had no memory of hearing. I'm old enough so that when a patient's memory is different from mine, I'm far from assuming that I'm right. However occasionally, it would be something like *Ya know, we talked about this, those abortions.* There turned out to have been one in high school and another in her mid-20s. Another example of something I'm pretty sure I would have remembered was *You know, remember I told you about the time I was suspended for cheating.* Of course, it's hard to know for sure but, when we discussed it, Barbara was convinced that her memories of telling me such things came from having imagined it.

If she was right, this too may be explained by the dominance of her right brain. The immersion in the imagined scene of telling me, the right brain picturing of it, and the coloring supplied by her strong affects may have given the fantasy a real seemingness that, in retrospect, could be confused with events that actually occurred. Barbara was fascinated by this. She came to realize that she was often hurt by someone not remembering something that she'd thought she'd told them. It confirmed her expectation of not being valued by them. She also realized that starting with "you know, I told you about ..." and then quickly telling them what she thought she had already told them was defensive, anticipating not being remembered. But my point here is about the vividness of her inner world. This is an example of a downside, but, of course, a vivid imagination is also a great strength.

Let's now move on now to discussing how Barbara's regulatory difficulties interfere with her capacity for intersubjectivity, agency, and self-generation.

Intersubjectivity: Whereas Ken was ill-equipped and ill-disposed to detecting and assessing his own and others' internal states, Barbara seemed born to the project. She was acutely sensitive to her own affects and to implicit expressions of affects coming from others. Whereas Ken was afraid of it, she loved and thrived on the experience of intimacy generated by real-time affect attunement. At the reflective-verbal level, she loved swimming around in her own and others' inner worlds. The stumbling blocks were, as already discussed, her susceptibility to misattribution, and, I would add, insufficient doubt about her assessments of her own and others' subjective experience.

Let's start with misattributions as an impediment to intersubjectivity. Intersubjectivity requires not only attending to one's own and others' affect states, but it also requires that the assessment is reasonably accurate. We've already encountered Barbara's reliance on projection of blame as a defense against shame. We also saw her questionable interpretation of Peter's daughter's intentions due to teleological reasoning. There was also a measure of egocentrism involved. She tended to think others were like her when an appreciation of differences was required. For example, I was surprised to find that it was a bit of a revelation for Barbara to consider that when Peter's daughter spent time in her bedroom, she might be seeking privacy. Barbara would have stayed around because of her own needs, not the least of which was to take care of the other person who she assumed would be hurt if she didn't hang around.

Recall that this ended with Barbara feeling rejected and angry and is a textbook case of failing to appreciate others as separate centers of subjective experience, the basic maxim of intersubjectivity. Until she discussed it with me, Barbara never questioned her interpretation of Peter's daughter's intentions, indeed never considered it to be an interpretation. Of course, she knew everyone was not the same, so what had happened?

My guess is that when thinking about her relationship with Peter's daughter, Barbara would enter a state of hyper-aroused dysregulation and thus extreme right brain dominance, i.e. subject consciousness without the objectification and skepticism provided by her left brain. Her need for objectification was one of the reasons she relied on dyadic regulation. *Peter can talk me down off the ledge just by listening. He never says, "calm* down." *People have said that to me all my life. I hate it. Peter listens to me and I can listen to him. It gives me a little distance from what I'm saying.* Peter connects to her and regulates her (calms her) allowing for the activation of the left brain and its objectifying processes.

Agency: Whereas Ken's agency was compromised by over-inhibition and his inclination toward inaction, Barbara's agency suffered from insufficient inhibition and her bent toward activation. Like Ken she was easily dysregulated and thus often without the capacity to process her affect, formulate her intentions, and act accordingly. The difference is that Ken's regulatory deficiencies result in failures to act, whereas Barbara's result in actions she regretted. Discussing a spat she had with a close friend…*I didn't mean it. It just came out. I actually had thought about it and decided not to say it and then I said it anyway. Even as I said it, there was something in the background nagging at me not to.*

There is, of course, a big upside to Barbara's hyper-aroused bias. She was high-spirited with a multitude of enthusiasms going at once, an astonishing number of which she saw through to completion. She didn't seem to be indifferent to anything and had abundant energy. At a celebration with friends upon graduation from medical school, she was given an award for "Most Indefatigable." She planned well into the future, leading her life proactively and fully. *I feel best when I have a lot going on. Sometimes it's too much, but there always seems to be room for one more.* She chose emergency medicine partly because *When work is done, it's done. You get to have a life.* She also liked it because *I'm in my element. I feel needed and it's intense. I come home exhausted, but in a good way.*

On the downside, Barbara's sympathetic autonomic bias rendered her vulnerable to impulsive and compulsive behaviors. We've probably seen impulsivity demonstrated in her brief first marriage and her unwanted pregnancies. We definitely saw it in her saying things that "just came out." Recall that agency includes whether one speaks or not, and whether one has command over what one says and how one says it. This was not Barbara's forte.

Along with speaking impulsively, Barbara was also vulnerable to speaking compulsively. *I can't believe what happened this weekend. It was humiliating. I don't learn! We had dinner with an old friend of Peter's who he has great respect for. I'd never met him and was late which made it worse. By the time I got there I was a wreck. I started talking before I even sat down. Everything was happening so fast. I can barely tell you what I was saying, just trying to get him to think I was clever, to like me. At one point I even got a glimpse of what was happening but just kept on going. I'm an idiot (crying).* Badly dysregulated, her anxiety running the show, Barbara had lost possession of herself and just talked. *I only came to my senses when Peter took my hand.*

Self-generation: As with Ken, I can only speculate about Barbara's difficulties with self-generation. I draw from her experiences with me as she attempted to process her stream of consciousness. Like Ken, her capacity for processing her stream of consciousness is impeded by becoming dysregulated-dissociated at low levels of stress and by an incapacity to process shame. However, Barbara has an option he doesn't have. Whereas Ken shies away from attunement and is unable to reap the rewards of dyadic states of consciousness, Barbara is capable of, indeed seeks out shared states. Also, when her relational attachment patterns don't interfere, and when she doesn't just use it for venting, she can make good use of dyadic processing of issues of concern.

Barbara's difficulties with self-generation lie in the autonomous processing of her stream of consciousness. Whereas Ken's stream is hypoactivated, Barbara's is hyperactivated. Whereas Ken avoids thinking about his issues of concern, Barbara can't keep her attention away from hers. She is often dysregulated by the thoughts that bubble up and is unable to think productively about them. And, of course, her thinking about interpersonal concerns was compromised by misattributions. However, the most formidable obstacle to self-generation was her incapacity to process shame.

Summary and Conclusion: In this book, I have proposed a model of mind organized by affect. I depict implicit and explicit states of consciousness and their coordination and argue that such states are affect state dependent. I also attempt to integrate Schore's conception of the implicit self with that of the reflective-self and thereby provide a model of the full self equipped with primary and secondary systems. I explore the primary and secondary systems for intersubjectivity, agency, and self-generation. Finally, I argue that states of consciousness and self-functions operate optimally when affect is regulated and become disordered when affect is dysregulated.

In this final chapter, I hope to have made the abstractions of the model come to life. I've used the model to describe my experiences with patients suffering from the sequelae of two types of early attachment trauma. Ken's avoidant trauma resulted in a parasympathetic bias which disposes him to states of consciousness marked by detachment and lacking in awareness of his own and others' subjective experience. It also resulted in socio-emotional inhibition, distant and overly accommodating object relations, deficient agency due to passivity, and a self-generative system that is underdeveloped and blocked from use by avoidance of stressful thoughts. Barbara's preoccupied trauma resulted in enmeshed and overly assimilative object relations, and in a bias toward hyper-arousal. This sympathetic bias resulted in insufficient affective inhibition and a proclivity for action. She was vulnerable to overly subjective and fragmented states of consciousness. Her considerable capacity for intersubjectivity was marred by misattributions, her impulsivity interfered with her agency, and her capacity for self-generation was hindered by dysregulation at low levels of stress and by misattributions.

Index

For Product Safety Concerns and Information please contact our EU
representative GPSR@taylorandfrancis.com
Taylor & Francis Verlag GmbH, Kaufingerstraße 24, 80331 München, Germany

www.ingramcontent.com/pod-product-compliance
Ingram Content Group UK Ltd.
Pitfield, Milton Keynes, MK11 3LW, UK
UKHW022321111225
465992UK00009B/129

* 9 7 8 1 0 3 2 2 1 0 7 3 5 *